ENCOURAGING CREATIVITY
IN ART LESSONS

ENCOURAGING CREATIVITY IN ART LESSONS

George Szekely

TEACHERS
COLLEGE
PRESS

Teachers College, Columbia University
New York and London

Published by Teachers College Press, 1234 Amsterdam Avenue,
New York, NY 10027

All photos by George Szekely of artwork by the author. He would like to acknowledge
the following exhibitors for displaying his work: Boston Artist's Union Gallery, Boston,
MA, 1978 (p. 99); Center for Contemporary Arts, Lexington, KY, 1985 (pp. vii, 141);
Contemporary Art Gallery, New York University, New York, NY, 1983 (p. 105); Kleinart
Gallery, Woodstock, NY, 1980 (p. 24); The Roundtower, Copenhagen, Denmark,
1979 (p. 162); Westbroadway Gallery, New York, NY, 1972, 1977, 1978, 1980, 1982
(pp. 2, 8, 48, 68, 90).

Library of Congress Cataloging-in-Publication Data

Szekely, George E.
  Encouraging creativity in art lessons.

  Bibliography: p. 185
  Includes index.
    1. Art—Study and teaching (Elementary)—United
States.   2. Art—Study and teaching (Secondary)—United
States.   3. Creative thinking (Education)   I. Title.
N353.S94   1988   707'.1273   87-25679
ISBN 0-8077-2883-7 (pbk.)

Manufactured in the United States of America

93 92 91 90 89 88   1 2 3 4 5 6

Contents

Preface   vii

1. **The Goals of Art Education: The Student Artist**   1

   Teaching Methods in Art   1
   Searching for Art: A Contemporary Art-Teaching Model   7
   Trying on the Artist's Role   16
   Conclusion   20

2. **Introducing Students to the Art Process**   23

   Students as Independent Artists   23
   Planning an Artwork as an Important Step
       in the Art Process   26
   Environmental Search   28
   Investigation of Materials   34
   Show and Tell: Sharing Everyone's Finds   37
   Sketchbooks   38
   Experimentation   43
   Time Management   44

3. **Creating a Classroom Environment**
   Favorable to Artistic Learning   47

   Material Design   51
   Display   55
   Classroom Design   61
   Play   67
   Performance   89

4. **Planning the Lesson**   **97**

    Selecting the Idea for the Lesson   100
    Selecting the Play Idea   102
    Visual Lesson Planning   103
    Sources of Lesson Ideas   106
    Timing and Sequencing   115
    Planning for Independent Work   118
    Planning for Discussions in Art   122
    Studying Other Artists and the Art World   124
    Ending the Lesson   126
    Evaluating the Lesson as a Work of Art   132
    Four Sample Lessons   133

5. **Evaluation and Recognition of Student Performance**   **139**

    Evaluating One's Own Work   140
    Using Art to Evaluate Art   148
    Getting a New Perspective   152
    The Art Exhibit as a Teaching Tool   153

6. **The Artist-Teacher**   **161**

    Becoming an Artist-Teacher   161
    The Teacher as Mentor and Colleague   166

Afterword   **173**

Appendix A: Content of Conversation in Art Classes   177

Appendix B: Printed Resources   180

Appendix C: Shopping Sources   183

Bibliography   **185**

Index   **191**

About the Author   **199**

Preface

This book describes an innovative approach to public school art education at the primary and secondary levels. The teaching philosophy here is the result of my fourteen years of teaching art to children in public schools (as well as to adults of all ages and educational backgrounds) and of my twelve years of teaching art education to college students. These ideas have evolved gradually from what I have learned from children themselves, from my experience with my own art, and from the teaching experiments that my graduate students and I have made together in the public schools.

Many of the ideas in this book surprise even me, for they differ from what I was taught about teaching art in my own college art education courses and from what I thought about teaching when I started out. When I began teaching art to children in 1971 fresh out of graduate school, I tended to think of children's art as a developmental stage on the way to something superior—adult art. Because my first students happened to be non-English-speaking children, however, I could not use with them the traditional, verbal teaching techniques I had been taught in graduate school and so the children and I communicated mostly through art. I learned to make art with them while the children created markings next to, on top of, under, and as extensions of communications between us. To my surprise, I simply fell in love with children's art, finding it something that I was drawn to for itself— in fact, some of the most exciting and honest art I knew. It was like Picasso's finding African art—discovering a whole different art world—except that, as a teacher, I was not only an observer of artifacts but a daily participant in their making. Eventually children's art replaced abstract expressionism as the major influence in my own professional work, and in my gallery shows, I successfully exhibited work that the children and I had made together.

Tablecloth and scroll paintings.

This was certainly a surprising development. I had assumed that it was my role to show the children how to make art—not vice versa. I had thought that the students would be learning from me—never imagining that I would learn so much from them. It also became apparent that the nonverbal techniques I had learned to use with the children who did not speak English worked well with children who did speak English (and that they were not part of the standard classroom approach). I even found that I was beginning to think of my students as fellow artists and colleagues—an idea that I certainly never encountered in graduate school.

To this point, my main knowledge of children was from school. Then, in my eighth year of teaching, I became a parent. Watching my children make art at home was the next major influence on my teaching. I not only became more convinced than ever of children's ability to make art, but now saw at firsthand the special world that produces children's art. Because I understood my own children's preoccupations at home—how important a lunchbox, a birthday party, a balloon could be—now, as a student of the children's world, I began to understand how these interests related to the art that children made in school. As a parent, I learned to appreciate my children's playful movements, inventive name calling, unusual arrangements of objects, and—most important—to see that these were as much a part of art making as the lines or color patterns in a picture. I was witness to how creative play with sand, bubbles, or cream cheese ended up in a sketchbook, or how arrangements of dolls, soldiers, or rocks became three-dimensional artworks. I watched as the children made things with bubblegum, stones, and worms (media that I never took courses in), adapting techniques from cooking, house cleaning, and dental care that adult artists have yet to invent. I listened as they freely and joyfully discussed their discoveries and artistic problems with anyone who would listen. Often, with great enjoyment, we made things together, but it was humbling—and enlightening—to realize that they were making their best things without me. They had, of course, my enthusiastic support for their explorations, and they also had the example of a working artist in the home as well as a very permissive parental attitude toward what materials are appropriate for art; but they seemed to work best when I stood back and let them make things on their own.

All of the "art" activities that the children engaged in when they worked independently had their parallel, it seemed to me, in the working habits of adult artists. Professional artists take pride in discovering their own ideas for art, regarding innovation as essential and imitation as deadly. An important school of modern artists, the Dadaists, regarded anything in the environment as suitable for art making and stressed that the techniques for art making must continually be reinvented. In their view, the traditional techniques, media, and tools formerly prescribed for art making no longer define the boundaries of art, for the boundaries no longer exist.

Adult artists demand the time and freedom to experiment at length with tools and materials as an art idea slowly becomes a finished work (or series of works). They insist that many types of "non-art" activities—behavior that other people regard as playing or loafing, such as gazing out of the window or going for a walk—are essential parts of the creative process, in which they are thinking about art ideas. They feel a need to talk with fellow artists about their ongoing work and about art in general, finding that as they talk they are not only learning new ideas but refining their current projects. A supportive audience of interested observers is vital to their work, and they feel a need to belong to a larger community of artists, an "art world."

If the way I saw my children making art on their own resembled the working methods of adult artists, however, there was a sharp contrast between these working methods and the way I knew that children are expected to make art in school. In the traditional approach to art education, the teacher usually chooses the idea for the art work in advance and introduces it to the class, through lecture and demonstration. The teacher also selects the materials and tools (often a carefully limited collection, allowing the children little choice). The art idea assigned is frequently a traditional technique or a simplified project that has been thoroughly tested in advance, so that it will present no problems. Most class time is taken up with the teacher's lecture and demonstration and with the children's making the assigned artwork. Little time is left for exploring the children's own art ideas, for experimenting with materials and tools, or for inventing new techniques. I was disturbed by the fact that so much of the school art that I saw seemed uninspired and imitative, a seeking to duplicate what the teacher presented to the students.

In watching my own children, I had learned what kind of help they needed with art making. They did *not* need me to think up ideas for projects, to select materials or tools for them, to demonstrate the specific techniques they would use, or to supervise the progression of a work from idea to finished product. Apparently my most important function was to serve as both an appreciative and supportive audience for their art and to be a model of the adult artist.

It was natural for me to begin changing my teaching style at school accordingly. Instead of thinking of myself as the source of knowledge about art, I began to think of myself more as a catalyst or change agent, whose primary function was to create conditions that inspired children with their own ideas for making art. At times I was a magician or an actor, devising props, scenery, and dramatic events to transform the classroom into a visually exciting place to be, or introducing materials and demonstrating techniques in unexpected ways, designed to stimulate the imagination. My lesson plans were now artfully hidden, not a uniform task set for all to do, but something designed to pose an art question—a new sight to see, a new way to play, a new form of interaction—that might start the children off on personal voyages of exploration. Avoiding the authoritarian role, I attempted to function as a supportive and sympathetic audience for the children's art and to share my own art with them, bringing my latest discoveries and enthusiasms with me into the class for them to share. I presented myself now to my students not as the one who "knows how to do art" but as a fellow artist, always himself in the position of discovering how art is made—for that is what I truly felt myself to be, and that is how I conceive of art: as something that is constantly being reinvented and rediscovered.

I have found that when children experience in art class a supportive environment that offers challenging visual experiences, and the example of an adult artist-teacher, and where the emphasis is put on experimentation, inviting children to invent their own art ideas, plan their own works, and investigate art techniques themselves, children not only produce impressive, original artworks but also learn about art in a much broader sense, coming to understand how artists work, how artists evaluate their works, how artists teach themselves about art, and the value of art as a way of life.

The innovative approach to teaching described in this book is not a formula or a set of techniques. Although it implies that changes in the traditional art curriculum are desirable, this approach is not in itself dependent on a particular curriculum or art program but on the creativity of individual art teachers. Although stronger financial and moral support for art from school systems and communities could make the task much easier, the kinds of innovations described in this book can be done—and have been done, in experimental research programs in the schools that are described in this book—within the limitations of the public schools as they are today. The heart of this teaching approach is the belief that the essential goal of art teaching is to inspire children to behave like artists—to try on the artist's role—to feel what it is to gather an art idea on one's own and act on it. The goal is to reveal to children that art comes from within themselves—not from the teacher. The goal is to demystify art, and assure children, through the teacher's deeds and words, that art is found in familiar places and ordinary environments, accessible to everyone. It is to bring children closer to art—nearer to themselves, to their own views and visions.

If each child is to fully experience what it is to be an artist, he or she needs to be treated like one. If we do not think of, talk to, and plan for our students as we would for artists, then we are merely giving them assignments to do and our own ideas to mimic. The authoritarian model of the teacher as one who "knows" all about a subject contradicts the message we want to give children about art—that art is, above all, a means of discovery. The model that students most need is the model of the artist; the most valuable resource that the art teacher brings to class is his or her *complete* artist self. To allow exposure of oneself—to permit students to see the teacher as an artist as openly and fully as possible—is part of the challenge of art teaching. Such self-presentation is not just a matter of "being yourself" or "doing your thing," of course; it requires careful thought, preparation, and planning.

The most essential requirement for art teaching is not mastery of specific artistic techniques or of traditional educational methods. The truly necessary credential is individual creativity of the kind that artists possess. It is the artist's unique vision that shines through the mundaneness of the everyday school routine. It is the artist's trained eye and focused imagination that can draw an artistic response from students. The ability to question, to doubt, and to look to ourselves for answers—a quality that artists have in abundance—provides the most exciting experiences to be shared with students, and the more involved teachers are with their own art, the deeper their insights reach into the art processes of others.

In talking with the experienced art teachers who take my graduate courses, I have learned that many of them feel teaching has denied them an outlet for their artistic creativity. It has become just a job, which lacks the challenge and excitement that initially drew them to art. Some, finding that the demands of teaching leave them too exhausted to do much work of their own, resent teaching, blaming it for depriving them of the challenging and fulfilling careers they dreamed of. Others have found time to go on making their own art, but they have kept it to themselves, separate from their teaching. Most of the teachers I talk with—whether or not they are discontented with teaching—look at art and teaching as separate enterprises. The concept of "artist-teacher" sounds strange to them.

If teachers think of their own art as something that must be kept at home, they are depriving themselves of one of their most valuable resources for teaching. Our ability to get students involved with art often depends on our success in letting them share in our own artistic journeys, for that is an essential part of the experience of learning from other artists. When we ourselves are making art daily, our observations and discoveries can be presented in class with the excitement of recent finds. Art making is necessary not only for ourselves as artists but also for our teaching. The cherishing of artistic freedom, independence, playfulness, and the opportunity to dream can best be cultivated in others when we have not left it far behind ourselves.

Many of us acquired the idea in graduate school, without being aware of it, that teaching and art are separate things. A split between art and education is clearly expressed in the structure of most college art education programs, where students usually study in three different departments. In the art department, studio classes are emphasized. In the education department, general teaching skills are studied. The art education department then attempts to tie the two approaches together.

In the art department, students learn to visualize, play, invent, communicate visually, and act intuitively themselves, but without enough reference to teaching these abilities to others. Studio classes in art education are supposed to address such issues more directly, but instead they often convey the unspoken message that only simplified, pretested projects are appropriate for children and that art ideas come from the teacher. In the education department, on the other hand, education is taught without enough reference to art. Students study the same techniques that are used for teaching other subjects. Little attention is given to the fact that art is not like most other school subjects. Most subjects are primarily concerned with traditional knowledge; art making is concerned with making an original response to immediate experience. Most school subjects can be learned best through verbal communication, but although verbal learning is very important in art, visual communication— which appears to have its own sequence and pattern and to differ significantly from verbal learning—is of greater importance. There is often a lack of communication among university teachers, especially between studio art teachers and art education teachers. Art education departments have in general not been sufficiently concerned about the "split" between art and education to resolve the problem. No one raises one of the most important professional issues that young teachers will have to face: how to preserve themselves as artists within the schools.

When I first tell the experienced teachers in my art education courses that they can behave like artists in school, they usually respond, "That sounds wonderful, but it isn't realistic. You don't know the conditions in the schools!" Then I tell them that I know the conditions all too well, because I have been working in the public schools for years—and that, in fact, the innovative teaching experiments we will be doing together will be specifically designed to find imaginative solutions to these very unfavorable conditions. How can a teacher arouse a child's sense of visual beauty in a drab and ugly classroom? How can we find interesting materials and tools to use in art making when we are chronically short of funds and supplies? How can we encourage the independence, playfulness, and originality that artists need when the school atmosphere conditions children to conform and to obey orders? How can we give children the freedom they need to play and explore the environment around them when traditional ideas of discipline prohibit much "playfulness" in school? How can we convince children that art can be important in their own lives when the community around them has so little respect for art and artists?

All of these are among the challenges that an innovative program in the schools is designed to meet. Many examples of techniques that my students and I have successfully experimented with to cope with these conditions in the public schools are described in this book. They are offered, however, not as a menu prescribing standard fare for the classroom, but as a sample that I hope will encourage art teachers to invent their own recipes (and write their own books). The essential ingredient in bringing about change in the schools is the willingness of artists-teachers to apply their individual creativity to the task.

This book is sent as a message to my artist-teacher colleagues to tell them that each one of us has an important role to play in our field— for art teaching has yet to be invented. What art teaching most requires is search, discovery, and invention—and there is room enough for all inventions. It is the artist in each of us that allows us to act as unique individuals with special contributions to make to the school. Learning to teach is learning to bring our most complete artist selves to bear on the task of teaching. As artist-teachers, we can begin to think of teaching as an art medium—to plan, present, and evaluate art lessons as artworks, and to view the content and outcome of our work in the light of contemporary art, the reality of the artist, and the art process.

ENCOURAGING CREATIVITY
IN ART LESSONS

1

The Goals of Art Education: The Student Artist

For many years, when I was teaching art to junior high school students on Staten Island, I held the first class of the year on the ferryboat that goes to New York City. The assignment was to sketch the city skyline as the boat moved across the New York Harbor. It never failed: Soon after the students began working, they were surrounded by crowds of curious passengers who responded excitedly to their drawings, asking questions and offering praise or criticism. In no time at all my students, most of whom were far from experienced artists, were discussing their drawings as though they had been making art for years. They explained why they were sketching a certain way, described their ideas, and eagerly defended their work against passengers' criticisms. Finding that others took their art seriously had given them the confidence to begin to think and work like artists—to try on the artist's role—and, in doing so, to begin to discover the artists within themselves.

We cannot always take students on field trips. We can, however, create in the classroom a stimulating environment in which students are challenged to create art, and an atmosphere in which students are taken seriously as artists, so that they themselves begin to feel and act like artists.

TEACHING METHODS IN ART

The traditional method of art teaching that is still widely used in many classrooms today, although it is intended to teach children how to make art, actually works against this goal in many respects. In 1984, I decided to make a study of how art teachers design and present their lessons, to confirm the impressions that I had gathered over the years by teaching and observing art teachers in the public schools in New

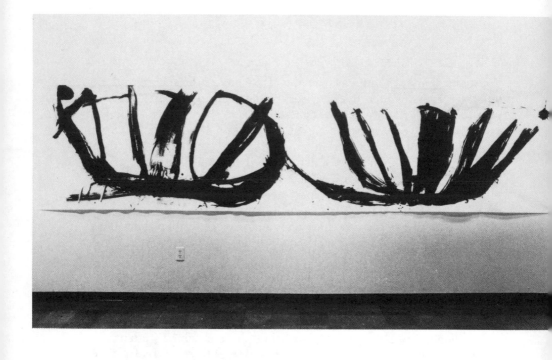

*Painted forms series: Reflections based
on a child's first paintings.*

York City and Lexington, Kentucky. The study, which took three years, focused on lesson planning by art teachers in grades 3 through 12 and on the responses of their students. I wanted to find out what planning strategies teachers used and how they noted them; I also wanted to compare the plans with what was actually done in class. More specifically, I wanted to know what areas of decision making were left to students. Ten art teachers in five elementary and five secondary schools were studied, with the aid of research assistants who were apprenticed to the teachers.

The study revealed that each teacher kept detailed, written lesson plans, which formed the framework of class instruction. The teachers faithfully duplicated in class the procedure described in their plans. Materials selection, demonstrations, lectures, instructions, and teachers' comments were used to introduce the lesson and to guide students through a teacher-prescribed experience. Lesson plans not only described the major concepts to be presented but were prescriptive as well; much, if not most, of the creative decision making was controlled by the teacher. The lesson plans not only presented a general concept but also dictated the specific experiences to be used in exploring that concept. It would be safe to say that because the art teachers in each class were responsible for most of the creative decision making, the artworks, and therefore the students' understanding of the nature of art, were narrowly limited.

In 88 percent of the lessons studied, the art teacher selected the materials, supplies, spaces, and themes beforehand and then carefully directed the process of making the works. Over 90 percent of the time, evaluations, criticisms, and directions given during the class did not come from the students in response to their work, but were statements made by the teachers reinforcing their initial objective as stated in their lesson plans. Numerous follow-up discussions between the research assistants and the teachers indicated that teachers generally perceived the artworks produced as illustrations of their plans, frequently referring with pride to successful projects as if they were their own works. Lessons judged successful by the teachers were those that managed to accomplish the teachers' plans. This last finding reminds me of an incident that occurred in one of my art education courses. A student who had been practice teaching for a few weeks came to me in tears, terribly distressed because one of the children was not doing the lessons she had planned. "I plan my lessons in detail every week," she sobbed, "and I know exactly what I want my children to do. I'm sure each lesson is valuable and fun—but I have a child who simply turns his back on whatever I suggest. All he wants to do is draw and paint!"

She went on to describe a child whom I had thought would be especially exciting to work with because of his unusual ability to concentrate and the large volume of impressive work that he had produced. My student complained that he did not want her lessons but preferred to work on his own. "I don't know how to get him to do the projects I plan!" she cried. Another graduate student who was listening to the conversation remarked perceptively, "I wish I had your problem! I have a child who doesn't lift a finger unless I ask him to. He won't make a line unless I reassure him that it's exactly what I want."

To return to the study: We found in examining recordings of interviews and anecdotal statements of observations that the students in these classes had little understanding of how teachers came to decide on specific lessons or why the prescribed experiences were valuable to pursue. More important, although students knew whether a work was successful or not—for this depended on whether the teacher liked it or not—they had little insight into their own work. They could not say what they had learned from it or how to apply their experience to new works. Ninety-seven percent of the time, students had little or no warning regarding the content of a lesson before they entered the art room and therefore spent no significant time preparing for their work physically, materially, or conceptually. Lessons were sprung on them at the beginning of each class, and they generally responded by following the teacher's directions without planning, preliminary investigation, or interpretation of what they had been told. They simply followed first impressions; the crucial time needed for the formation of ideas, opinions, and plans was seldom provided for in these classes. Little account was taken of the fact that artworks do not appear from nowhere, on the spur of the moment, but grow slowly, out of many different personal experiences of the environment, and need time to develop.

Planning and Preparation in Making Art

When teachers assume that students can make artworks simply by following instructions, they are forgetting how important *thinking about art ideas* and *preparing for the artwork* are in the art process. Artists prepare for art making by thinking about their ideas, visualizing the works they might make, recording ideas in notes and sketches, planning for the works, searching for materials, and playfully experimenting with various possibilities for carrying out the ideas. Lessons that place the major emphasis on following instructions and learning set techniques of art making do not come to terms with the basic problem of introducing students to the artistic process. Time has to be found *within* the lessons to help students prepare for art making by responding to experience of the environment, thinking about art ideas, and making the other essential preparations. Also, since there can never be enough time within the period for adequate preparation for art making, lessons must be designed to motivate students to use their own time *outside* of art class—not only at home but during all sorts of daily experiences—to prepare for art making by seeing, thinking, and responding as an artist does.

Teachers devise rigid lesson plans as an efficient means of presenting information to a large group of people. Obviously, a lesson devised for a mass audience has its shortcomings. It assumes that all students have the same interests, capabilities, and needs and respond with the same enthusiasm to the same experiences. It offers the same presentation to everyone, whether interested or not. Yet art can only be made when the artist is excited about an idea and hence committed to it. When teachers specify exactly how the artwork is to be made they impose their view of art on their students. The teacher may proclaim a belief in individualism in art, but if the class is set up as the teacher's "production line," with students working from the same instructions and using the same tools and materials, there is little chance for choice and hence for individuality. When, on the other hand, students base their works on their own experiences, dreams, and values presented in terms of their own images, individuality is evident in each work. The teacher cannot present a standard response to the works, reflecting and reinforcing his or her own views, but must give specific responses, tailored to the goals of each student.

When students are dependent on the teacher, they are not committed to their work, and initiative is lost. They look to the teacher for guidance in selecting subjects, tools, materials, and processes; they need the teacher's assistance to complete a project and to move from project to project. It becomes increasingly difficult for them to work independently, to assert themselves without direction and reassurance from the teacher. The lesson is thus totally unlike the creative process as experienced by artists. Artists make their own decisions, indeed, often agonize over them, and they are not assured that they will succeed in the end. The artist profits from the possibility of failure in perhaps having to redirect a work. The student has no such option. The typical art lesson is designed so that by simply completing it, students will succeed —succeed, at least, in expressing the purposes of the teacher.

Students should be involved from the beginning in planning their artworks. The first "problem" for them to solve is determining the art problem itself that is to be worked out in the project. Artists learn to see their own problems, and students should do the same. Solving the problems of others does not inspire in us the same enthusiasm as uncovering our own. Thus, a major aspect of art education is giving students the responsibility for learning, that is, for searching out, formulating, and examining their own ideas, for recognizing possible solutions, and for choosing the materials and techniques needed to pursue them.

The making of a work of art begins with the development of art ideas, based on a wide range of experience and the consideration of materials. In school it is usually the teacher who selects the art idea. Teachers believe that in doing so not only will the students understand the lesson clearly and begin actual manipulation of the materials efficiently but that they will also be spared the "frustration" of the art-making process: searching for ideas; looking at art; deciding on materials, tools, forms, moves, and the play that can begin the visualization of an idea in the artist's mind. As a result, when students enter the room, only the teacher knows what will take place during the class. The teacher unloads a continuous string of surprises on the students for which they are not necessarily prepared. The students are not left any choice; all the creative concepts have already been mapped out. Yet the preliminary planning of an artwork, the search for ideas and materials and playful experimentation with materials and techniques, are integral parts of the creative process.

An art lesson should provide students with the opportunity to observe and react to a variety of experiences. Students must feel that there are possibilities beyond what is conveyed to them by the lesson: art still to be made and fresh ideas to be welcomed. Students must learn how and where to find ideas, how to formulate and preserve them, and how to gather the resources that will best express them. They must learn how artists explore what is unusual, beautiful, or interesting to them and how they utilize their finds. They must learn to do all this on their own, not only in class on a given day or week, but out of class too, on every day of the week.

It will be hard for many of us art teachers to dispense with the belief, long held, that there is a certain fund of knowledge with which students should be familiar, and that instruction from the teacher is the most efficient means of receiving this knowledge. It will also be hard, in the words of Silverman, to "shake off all the mindlessness of current practices, old routines, time schedules, uniform lessons, teacher selection of lessons and materials" that have resulted from this belief.* We need to recognize that children are not blank slates coming to class without ideas, skills, or knowledge. Indeed, we need to consider what each child brings to class and how to build on that, instead of building on the "wisdom" of the art teacher and the art tradition. The aim of an art lesson, then, is to create a situation in which children can invent, and, as Piaget has said, discover structures and principles. We want to ensure that students will continue to generate their own ideas and act on them after their schooling is over. In this way we show that art is not just a body of special techniques used to produce school projects but something relevant—indeed, central—to our lives.

One critical measure of the success of art teaching is whether in our teaching we are working with the latest ideas of art *as they are currently understood in the contemporary art world.* In the next section I would like to briefly sketch for you my own model for contemporary art teaching, because it stresses ideas about art and art making that are very familiar in the art world but that do not receive enough emphasis in school art. This is the model that I will be working from throughout this book, and it explains some of the emphases in my teaching that may seem unusual at first but that are really quite familiar when we think of contemporary art.

SEARCHING FOR ART:
A CONTEMPORARY ART-TEACHING MODEL

If there is one thing that is certain about contemporary art, it is that the whole question of what art *is* is a major focus for the contemporary artist. To be an artist today is to be continually engaged in questioning what art is and what it could be; it is to be constantly reinventing art.

The outstanding feature of contemporary art is its openness to a diversity of styles and views, its willingness to call into question all traditional definitions of art and all established ideas of the nature of art making, the artist, and works of art. The boundaries that used to strictly separate painting from sculpture, or "works of art" from natural or manufactured objects, or the visual arts from music, literature, and dance, have disappeared. So has the idea that only certain sub-

*Silverman, Ronald H. *A Syllabus for Art Education.* Los Angeles: The Foundation, California State University, 1972. p. 8.

*Paintings on wallpapers and floor tiles, suggested by
collections of children's mixing trays, after painting.*

jects, materials, or tools are "proper" for art: The contemporary artist
feels free to look anywhere and everywhere in the environment for art
ideas, materials, and tools—including the local discount store, the fast-
food restaurant, among television or computer images. The commercial world, which used to be regarded as a wilderness where no art
could flourish, today is recognized as a rich source of art and art ideas,
and artists actively seek to learn from their colleagues in commercial
and industrial design, who have much to teach us about how human-
kind marks and alters the environment.

Instead of attempting to conceal the "object-ness" of works of art, contemporary artists often call attention to it. Both painting and sculpture have dealt with the issue of displaying themselves as objects. Paintings, for example, have become three-dimensional and architectural, not painted as illusions going into the canvas but as real forms staying on and "describing" the wall. Since the 1960s, contemporary artists have recognized that the materials of art are real substances in and of themselves, not just tools to be used to create illusions. A paint surface can simply be a paint surface; a canvas, fabric and wood; and the paint itself an exciting material to be selected and displayed for its own unique qualities. Art materials are regarded now as basic elements of artworks, not simply as common raw materials undeserving of attention or emphasis. For example, the consistency, amount, and color of paint make up a painting but also communicate something about the nature of paint itself; these qualities suggest how and where the paint is to be used and the various techniques that might be employed in executing the painting.

Thus, it is clear that our whole idea of what art is, and what it can be, is constantly being redefined today. The old "basics" for art teaching are out of date. The new basics, it seems to me—if teaching is to keep up with the art world—are exactly the sort of artistic *questions or issues* that I have just been mentioning: above all, the understanding that to be an artist today is to be constantly searching, experimenting, and rediscovering what art is and how it can be made, found, or discovered. If we offer our students anything less than this (a group of traditional formulas or recipes for art making, for example) we simply are not bringing them to art as it exists today.

Teaching individuals to engage in their own search for what art is and what it can be is the key to innovative art teaching. Art teaching is helping individuals to develop their own unique ideas. Promoting individual investigation must therefore be the center of importance in all of our teaching. Students need to be taught to take their own ideas and observations seriously and to turn to themselves first and foremost for solutions and answers. Art teaching needs to exemplify the process of independent research, the willingness to be different, and the ability to try new things. Students need to view art as a process of questioning and experimenting rather than one of looking for answers from the teacher or others. Art lessons, therefore, need to be stated in the form of questions, posing problems and presenting challenges, so that students can learn to seek their own solutions and become aware that new possibilities still exist. Making art, they must discover, is a process of sorting through possibilities. The contemporary art class does not have to be a place where an art project is made every period, but it will, ideally, be a place for observing and for sharing ideas, collections, and plans—a place to investigate, compose, suggest dreams, consider fantasies.

When teachers come to school, what we most need to bring with us in our shopping bags or supply carts is inspiration for art, for it is not already present in the sterile, uninspiring, and restricted elementary school classroom. Students' inner visions need to be encouraged, their bodies awakened, and their imaginations activated. Their sense of exploration, experimentation, and play needs to be licensed and encouraged. Teaching art deals with importing excitement and bringing beauty into the school in the form of new sights to see, new ways to play, new things to do. In many classrooms, exciting views and unexpected things to see and play with are termed "distractions." The teacher's solutions and plans dominate all activities. Art teaching needs to bring in jump ropes, hoola hoops, beach balls, and bubbles; to raise children's spirits, restore attention to their basic interest, invite movement and play, and thus let visions and artworks come to life.

Art teaching requires the ability to learn *from* children—to be a "kid observer," taking note of children's play, their dress, their language, even their snacks, so that school art can be based on what is meaningful to children, and contemporary. A wealth of teaching ideas can be gathered from simple observation of the natural dances children do during outdoor recess or the collections they bring to school in their pockets or lunch boxes (especially the ones that are smuggled into school but noted by the sharp-eyed art teacher).

Whereas most of school life deals with learning routines, the art class must present the extraordinary, the different, and the new, as it fits into an existing, ordinary world. Playfulness—which enables children and artists alike to reach beyond their ordinary selves and ways of thinking, to invent new ways of seeing, feeling, and being—must be licensed and encouraged in art class. We will know we are on the right track with our teaching if we find that when our students are working hardest at their art, they feel that they are playing. But playfulness and the invention of art ideas do not just "come about" in art class: They need to be invited and inspired by creatively planned art lessons and a teacher who also plays and invents art in class.

Art lessons need to be visualized, to be seen in the art teacher's mind as something beautiful, exciting, and inviting. They can be looked upon as the planning of an art performance and a creative contribution to inspire and invite others. Art lessons, however, are not *solutions or answers* that are the *demands of the teacher or to be enforced by the teacher*. Although a lesson can be a gift of a beautiful experience, one should not be so much attached to it that one cannot be ready to receive the student's innovations and extensions beyond the lesson plan. In fact, art teaching begins and does not end with the lesson's presentation, for it is then that the students' own plans and ideas, which modify the presented lesson, can be developed.

The original discoveries and observations that lead art teachers to decide on particular lessons are made outside of class. It is the *results* of these inspirations and discoveries that are shared with students in class. Students come to class with the same opportunities as the teacher, having found interesting ideas, having had important experiences, having collected something unusual that they can bring, as art and art ideas, to class. No matter how exciting the teacher's lesson is, the school environment can never be as inspiring to students as the possibilities for meaningful observations and experiences that exist outside of class. It is the art teacher's job to bring in beautiful things, to import collections and ideas—but also to train students to import substantial things from their out-of-school experiences to share with the teacher.

The range of art ideas that we present to even our youngest students will ideally be very broad. Just as contemporary artists must be aware of what is going on in the world of commercial art and design, so art teaching can range widely through the art environment of our time and culture, paying special attention to the art influences that are particularly important to children. Art teachers must feel free to look at everything, collect and surround themselves with beautiful forms from all media, and to demonstrate, in school, art inventions based on everything from music videos and fast-food containers to the packaging of a snack or a new board game. Children's play ideas and contemporary art ideas occur and can find expression in any medium. A color lesson may involve instruction in dance, painting with lights, or the display of images on television. Art is not a known commodity. It needs to be discovered and searched for everywhere and in everything.

Even at the beginning of the student's art experience, at the elementary school level, the elementary school artist is a *contemporary* artist, and the awareness of the relevance of the art environment of one's time and culture to one's own art can begin right there. As a contemporary artist, the elementary school student carries well-designed visual objects such as toys, lunchboxes, and prizes that are both an important part of the student's world and a resource for art.

Does the plastic Halloween mask from K–Mart really have any similarity to an African mask, or is it just contemporary "trash," generally ignored as a deposit of today's culture? In my view, it is the K–Mart mask, the Happy Meal box, that really reflect the ceremonies and interests of today's young warriors. K–Mart images, television-ad heroes, and the latest toys need to be taken seriously and used in art class. Children can develop a feeling for contemporary colors, for example, much more easily by examining new colors for toothpaste, nail polishes, or rainboots than by visiting an art-supply store. Adult artists take popular culture seriously and have made great art out of common things—what most people call "junk." A similar experience needs to be considered by children, using *their* interests and culture as the basis for art.

As contemporary artists, students also need to be encouraged to move beyond familiar things and to become fully open to art—that is, to *all kinds* of art and artists. Art teaching is training young people not to be afraid of new ideas but, on the contrary, to enjoy looking for new sights and experiences, in new forms. The essential of art learning is the ability to be curious about everything—what may be new in postcards, T-shirt designs, or museum exhibits. The art room, therefore, is the place where the "new" is welcomed, collected, and researched.

Students can learn in art class that they already know a great deal about art and that they know artists, too, who are all around them in the neighborhood—in the van-conversion shop, the interior designer's office, or back in the alley spraying graffiti—and that there really are artworks at the movie theater, the arcade, and the toy store. As contemporary artists, students need to learn to make connections and to see the relationships among familiar visual phenomena and all sorts of designed objects—to be aware that there is a continual dialogue going on among artists all around them, expressed in such familiar things as subway art or graffiti, and supermarket displays. Once they become aware of this, they can join in the dialogue themselves, bringing with them to school the Star Wars items, sticker books, or designer towels that can inspire their own artworks and those of others in the class.

Contemporary art students need to be keenly aware of how all professions and life activities change surfaces, leaving different marks on them through a variety of processes and materials. Our students need to be free to borrow a dental tool to draw with, to make believe that they are using a farmer's plow to cross an art surface, to utilize food mixers and blenders in inventing new colors, or to imitate the motions of playing Ping-Pong, as forms are moved from one side of the paper to another. From the simplest to the most complex environmental and life processes, from cleaning house to going shopping, one can become aware of countless tools and techniques and materials to be used for one's art, as well as how one's art forms, as environmental forms, can be stored, displayed, and interestingly presented. Contemporary art students also need to be free to work with technology and accept art on an Etch-a-Sketch or a video game screen, as well as to make art with lasers, spray guns, and computers.

Children can learn without distinction (as we really do in ordinary life) from all the arts, not just the visual arts. They can, for instance, be free to decide on a sculptural form after having danced it out through their own bodies in space, or to view dances as examples of moving sculpture, or to hear the sounds of a music synthesizer as examples of spacing, rhythm, and texture, or to explore visions for art through song, poetry, story, or personal writings. Multimedia, multisensory experiences that promote holistic involvement in learning can be the rule rather than the exception in art class.

When the teacher exhibits a broad interest in all types of art forms, students see how artists are able to extend themselves beyond their specialties and appreciate every kind of art—just as, for example, my musician friend who teaches classical piano can easily converse with my nine-year-old son about transformer music or the music on the soundtrack of a G.I.-Joe cartoon. The constant use of the broadest possible range of examples also lays the groundwork that allows us to draw children's attention *beyond* the areas they are already familiar with and to explore with them the relationships between their own art world and the work of contemporary artists. In studying the work of the geometric painters, for example, a teacher can also look at the work of contemporary kaleidoscope artists or the designers of magic cubes (different versions of Rubik's cube). Or, in the study of paints, one can include cosmetics, car paint, and furniture stain.

For contemporary artists, there will be less emphasis in art class on the physical construction of a work of art and more on finding art, planning art, and playing experimentally with art ideas and materials.

Finding art, discovering art, is a vital technique of being an artist today. With simple modifications or adaptations, or with no changes at all, found objects can be brought into new settings, new contexts, and presented to others as one's artistic discovery.

For example, a great deal of children's natural artistic production from their early years deals with what they frequently refer to as "setups." This is the art of utilizing ready-made objects, from toy soldiers to teddy bears, sometimes with the addition of home furnishings such as pots and pans, to create elaborate settings. The art of displaying or rearranging a world already existing of found objects or people is an important contemporary art form. A valuable learning area for the contemporary school artist is the continuation of this arrangement and display playing with all kinds of forms.

Although abstract expressionism has been wrongly interpreted in the schools as intuitive, spontaneous, yet mindless performing, recent trends toward a more thoughtful approach in the art world have brought back the balance between intuitive and planned art making. Finding art involves planning and thinking about art in the art class; talking about art and projecting art ideas must be of equal importance to the physical act of making art. School art needs especially to explore how art ideas are generated, how to harvest ideas, and how to keep records of them and select ideas on which to act. Planning needs to be considered an essential aspect of art making.

Traditional school art tends to rush children into art making and manipulation of art materials to complete their works too quickly, before they have had time to explore their ideas in their minds, their bodies, or their imaginations. Art class can instead be a place where children are encouraged to engage in preliminary experimentation and play *before* art making, so that they can develop their ideas. For example, before we begin painting on canvas, we can take time out to discover what a canvas is, and what it could be, examining the fabric and the wood that is used for the stretcher. After noting how a traditional canvas is constructed, students can then be encouraged to play with the fabric and the wood, assembling the frame and stretching or draping the canvas over various surfaces, which creates different support possibilities and gets them thinking about how different kinds of fabrics could be stretched, draped, or pulled over a variety of supports. We could also talk about and examine other materials that are of our contemporary life—plastics, floor tiles, wallpapers—as alternative canvases, and discuss the "canvases" we walk or ride on (floors, streets, highways). This element of awareness of what is known as art, and the playing out of many possibilities, with rethinking and questioning to find new solutions, can be part of each art lesson.

Exploring the nature of the canvas and the wood not only gives students time to plan and experiment but calls their attention to the work of art as an object and to art materials as constituent elements of the work. Students are used to playing with objects and can begin to pay more attention to the visual and surface qualities of objects they collect or play with. Classroom experiences can deal with the qualities of contemporary objects, the tools and processes for making them, and how they can be altered in size, material, and appearance, how they can be grouped or displayed and studied as artworks. Contemporary school art can become less involved with making art that is an illusion but give greater attention to finding, playing with, and creating artworks as objects. We should note that in the past, school art has dealt mostly with creating illusions of real things, using techniques such as perspective drawing and shading to present images of real objects convincingly on paper. Instead of making pictures of real objects, students can become more concerned with the objects themselves: For instance, instead of trying to make a picture of a chair look like the real thing, they can design chairs, stack chairs, paint on chairs, and wrap chairs.

When we paint in class, I do not encourage students to think of making a picture as creating an illusion, but to think about a real experience. For example, if they are painting flowers, I ask them to become the florist who is making a flower arrangement, or to act out the role of a gardener who is growing and displaying plants that are sprouting right out of the paper, and to imagine using tools and movements related to this task. For other paintings the paper may become a playing field, or a stage for a performance, or a battlefield, or a showcase, and I urge the children to move colors across the paper as though they were kicking a soccer ball across a field or bouncing a Ping-Pong ball back and forth, or displaying their colors and forms as baked goods in a showcase, or setting up toys—soldiers on a battlefield.

I describe the paper or canvas in different ways depending on its qualities and the kind of drawing or painting we are doing. If it is a long sheet of paper, I call it a runway; if it has a shiny surface, I call it a skating rink. Often, we start our drawing or painting with the students' tools lying on the table, as the children plan how to enter their stage, envisioning the moves to be made, and where to exit with the imaginary audience's applause. Then we take up our tools and enter as dancers, machine operators, or athletes and perform on our respective stages.

For sculpture, we take from children's play the idea of making setups, arranging everything—soldiers, dolls, teddy bears, cookies, valentines. Arrangements can be made on the floor, on a bed, inside a crib, or in a dollhouse, all of which can be thought of as art surfaces for sculptural settings or sculpture gardens. We also talk about sculpture displays of interest in the local environment—the sculpture that is set up and displayed at the butcher's, the baker's, or the fast-food restaurant. We discuss professionals who make sculptural designs: athletic coaches planning a game, choreographers coordinating the movement of dancers, police directing traffic—all are examples of ways of envisioning the arrangement of three-dimensional figures. Sculpture exercises also become practice for drawing and painting. Before we do two-dimensional artworks, my classes create all kinds of setups with three-dimensional objects, moving about Legos, ping-pong balls, soap pads, or marshmallows connected with sticks. The discoveries from the three-dimensional exercises are then recorded in their drawings and paintings.

Contemporary school artists can also learn to plan and consider artworks they may not be able to or wish to execute themselves. Planning works that are to be made by foundries, factories, or even robots is a legitimate form of making art. The act of choreographing and designing artworks to be carried out by others is an increasingly important procedure of contemporary artists.

In finding or making their art, contemporary school artists can move freely among the traditional art media, making drawings with sculptural materials, if they want to, or constructing three-dimensional paintings. Respected classical flutist James Galway speaks highly of the Beatles and actively records works of the Ragtime master Scott Joplin. Artists find inspiration across the boundaries of media working with a solid awareness of the underlying elements of their art—what connects media, how they overlap, and what separates them. The ability of visual artists to view contemporary dance as movements of sculptural color and form requires the understanding of the underlying elements such as form and color that exist across art media.

I will end this description of my model for art teaching by returning to what I said in the beginning. The art of today—the day I am writing this book, for example—will already be out of date by the time you read this sentence. Art is constantly being reinvented, and that is as true of the art in the classroom as it is of art anywhere. To teach art is no more, and no less, than to discover and learn with, and from, our students—the *really* contemporary artists—what art is and what it will be.

TRYING ON THE ARTIST'S ROLE

Our goal as art teachers, we have seen, is to help all of our students, from the youngest child in elementary school to the oldest high-school student, experience as fully as possible what it is to be an artist, to act and think like an artist, to try on the artist's role. What exactly does this mean? And how realistic is this goal, given the limitations of the public schools and the low status assigned to artists in our society?

The goal of helping all of our students to be artists will seem unrealistic and impossible, perhaps, if we start with the assumption that the ability to make art is rare. My own teaching, as I explained in the Preface, begins with the assumption that all children *are* artists, born with the natural ability to observe, to formulate art ideas, and to execute works of art on their own. Very young children make art on their own as a form of play. As children grow up, however, they come to depend on adults to direct their art making. In school, drawing is no longer a natural way of expressing oneself but part of something special called "the arts" that is taught by special teachers, using specialized materials. Because children no longer feel capable of expressing themselves naturally, of formulating ideas through art, they find it difficult—and they even fear—making art on their own. It is this fear of acting independently, of proceeding without being told what to do, that teachers must help children conquer. The first step in teaching children to make art is to be concerned that they regain their independence.

Teachers must convince each child that he or she possesses unique abilities—that art is to be regarded with confidence and pleasure as something all children are able to do in some way for themselves. When we offer children the freedom to play and experiment, their natural curiosity about the environment around them, their excitement about their own ideas, sensations, and feelings, and their desire to communicate these responses are strong motivations for making art. Such freedom can exist only when the adult artist in the class serves as a guide, model, fellow player, and mentor—not as an authority figure telling students what art is and exactly how to make it.

The teacher's motivation and level of self-confidence are important too. We are artists. If, when we come to class, we believe that we should tell children only a little of what we know about art and about being an artist, we will probably begin to feel frustrated. We will also be losing one of the most powerful teaching techniques available to us—using ourselves as examples of the artist. The goals of the artist-student and those of the artist-teacher are inseparable. If students do not have the freedom to behave like artists, then the teacher will not have the freedom to behave like an artist either—and if the teacher (the only adult artist present) is not acting like an artist, how can the children learn what an experienced adult artist is like?

A professional artist is not just a person who *makes* art: An artist is someone who thinks about art, talks about it, understands (and can discuss) the importance of art as a unique type of human activity, and who builds his or her life on it. An artist is also a critic, who understands the significance of works that he or she has made for the artist's own development and can apply what has been learned to future works. An artist is also an art historian, who values the works of earlier artists and learns from them. An artist is a student of the contemporary art world, keenly interested in new developments in art. An artist is also a worker, and the profession of art requires the same level of commitment, labor, and sacrifice as any other career—some would say, more. An artist has a particular social role, in both the specialized art world and the larger society. All of these things about being an artist are implied when I say that students need to try on the artist's role. Learning how artists make works of art is an important part of learning to be an artist, but it is only a part. Being an artist is a way of relating to society, a way of understanding oneself and the world, and indeed, an entire *way of life*. To understand what sort of life artists live—how being an artist affects your daily life, your income, your family, your social contacts, your emotions, your knowledge of the world, and your general approach to living—is part of trying on the role of the adult artist. If we want our students to have a genuine opportunity to consider art as a way of life for themselves and to have a realistic understanding of how artists live, we need to make them aware of all of these things.

Many children come to school already wanting to be doctors, mechanics, scientists, professional athletes, or businesspeople. They usually know people who do these jobs, which are not only highly visible but enjoy high social approval. They have some idea of the kind of work these people do. Artists are much less visible, and some adults disapprove of them, regarding them as people who play while others work. To many adults and to their children, the artist's world at best is distant and mysterious; they literally do not know what artists do or what their work involves. Some pleasurable art making in school, some museum trips and study of artworks from the past, and the mastery of some traditional art skills may give students a positive feeling about art, but such limited experiences are hardly likely to overcome the negative stereotypes many children have of the artist's life or to convince them that art is anything more than a pleasant pastime. The social attitudes toward art and artists that children bring with them to school can interfere with serious art making and prevent students from having a real opportunity to try on the artist's role, to consider art as a profession for themselves, or even to accept it as a valid profession for anybody. Students will not be able to feel real commitment to their work in art or to realize that it can have great personal value and meaning for them unless we are somehow able to overcome the powerful negative social stereotypes about the artist's life and work that they come to school believing. Art teachers need to venture boldly into the area commonly thought of as belonging to social studies and help students to understand the social role of artists and the nature of the art world.

When the art class is thought of as a community of artists (one of whom is an adult, and a professional artist), a perfect opportunity exists for sharing ideas about art and artists—discussing one's own and others' experiences of art making, talking about the nature of art and of artists, and discussing and examining the work of famous artists of the past and professional artists of the present. Being in art class implies a relationship with others as artists and as audience, others with similar joys and similar problems. It implies learning not only from our own work and from the teacher but also from others—including professional artists. Where do they get their ideas? How do they begin their work? How freely are they able to work? What do they carry over from one experience or work that helps with the next one? Do they have ideas that are similar to our own? How do they execute them differently? What can we discover, with the help of others, from the work we have just done? What would we never do again and why? What can't we wait to do the next time? These are questions that need to be talked about, explored, and tentatively resolved. When the focus of the art lesson is on art—not on specific techniques—such conversations occur quite naturally if the teacher encourages them, and the teacher also serves as a living example, sharing his or her own experience of art, the artist's life, and the art world with the children. In a social situation in which a group of people are making art together, it is not at all artificial to discuss the social experience and working lives of artists: It is not only relevant but, if students are encouraged to talk freely about what they are doing, almost unavoidable. Through conversation about artists and the art process, students can learn that many people make art and that there is an art community. In the process, many of the prevalent misconceptions about art and artists can be dispelled. Art is demystified for the children, and they learn how artists really work and how art is made.

Too often students get the impression in school that art is something you do once or twice a week, for an hour or so, when you make something in art class. Students do not realize how many other sorts of experiences and preparations go into the making of an artwork. They do not realize that the time that goes into actually making the artwork may be only a very small portion of the total time the artist spends on art. They do not know that being an artist also involves being aware of everyday experiences in a particular way, recording or remembering experiences, actively exploring the physical environment, continually seeking new ways of looking at or understanding the environment, thinking about planning and visualizing artworks projected from one's experiences of the environment, and many other "invisible" or subtle kinds of experience. They do not realize that artists can work at their art even when they are far away from their studios and art materials— that artists can be seeing with an artist's eye and thinking about art while to other people they seem to be doing nothing more than shopping at the supermarket, eating a hamburger at McDonald's, mowing the lawn, or visiting a new place when they go on vacation.

We need to teach students to build these sorts of artistic experiences into their own lives *outside of school and beyond the classroom.* Helping students to work independently in school and to produce original artworks in class is important, but it is not enough. The truly successful art lesson is one that inspires students to make their own artistic explorations outside the classroom and to begin to think and act like artists in their daily lives. Our designs for innovative art lessons are intended, then, to help students rehearse and practice the kinds of personal explorations they can make on their own, outside of class. From this point of view, art class is not the ultimate destination for our students' activity as artists but simply the launch pad, where we give them the impetus and direction to take off on their own.

CONCLUSION

The value of an innovative approach to art teaching for the individual student has been implied throughout this chapter. To make it possible for children to use natural abilities that otherwise would go unrecognized; to help children to integrate their sensory, emotional, and intellectual experience; to teach children to value their own personal feelings and ideas and to communicate them to others; to show children how to use their art making as a way of exploring and understanding the world around them and the nature of human life— this is clearly to fulfill the purpose of education for the individual. When individual students learn that their own ideas are of value—that they themselves are artists and that the things they make can have value for others—they achieve a new identity. The self-confidence and ability to work independently that they learn through their art making may well carry over into other activities and help them to approach other life tasks more confidently. Learning to approach any school subject as a form of active, analytical investigation—by observing, comparing, experimenting, evaluating, and reaching one's own conclusions—is excellent preparation for later school work and also for life after leaving school.

Society has need for individuals with such skills. Schools have always emphasized uniformity; it was felt in the past that if children were to fit into society, they must learn to march to its beat. But society's needs are changing; it no longer requires such uniformity. Education must catch up. Everyone emphasizes the value of computers for individualizing education, but few have realized that art instruction can play a key role in allowing the potential of each student to come forth. Art provides the diversified learning experience that students need to prepare them for the future. Society must take advantage of the best art education can offer: teaching individuals to assume their individuality.

2

Introducing Students
to the Art Process

In the first chapter, I suggested that a teacher-centered approach to art teaching is unsuited for teaching art because it contradicts the nature of art in crucial ways. I also suggested that the traditional focus of art lessons for children has been too narrow, concentrating too much on certain limited techniques and preventing us from dealing with how art is really made and what artists do. Our goal is to assist both students and teacher to function as artists in the classroom. What changes in our approach to teaching does this imply, and what, specifically, needs to be added to supplement the familiar classroom activities that have defined the nature of public school art learning in the past?

STUDENTS AS INDEPENDENT ARTISTS

A major change is the assumption that students will do their art projects independently, so that they can learn to work on their own, as artists do. This means that the individual student will be involved in the planning of the artwork from the beginning, choosing the art idea and materials (that is, identifying the art problem to work on); developing the idea by experimenting, playing it out in various forms, and discussing it with others; and constructing the work, making the crucial creative decisions about it. The teacher will not assign uniform projects in which everybody in the class makes exactly the same sort of thing at the same time, starting and finishing together. Instead of emphasizing a uniform learning experience, the teacher will identify areas of broad artistic concern within which individual students will be challenged to identify art problems with particular meaning for them. Supervising individual projects, of course, is more difficult in some respects than having everybody do the same project. It takes time and effort to get students going on individual projects, to plan for them to

*Shokan landscapes inspired by
children's rock garden sculptures.*

work outside of class, and to keep track of all of their individual projects. The rewards, in terms of their greater involvement and creativity, as well as the teacher's own creative involvement, make the effort worthwhile.

In addition to identifying broad areas of artistic concern for class lessons, the whole design of the lesson will be intended to challenge students to make art on their own. First and foremost, we need to think of each lesson as a form of play, and develop our lessons from children's own play ideas, so that kids in school can play and invent and use their own ideas as freely in school as they do when they are playing at home. By learning from the children what are the play ideas that inspire them, we can design art lessons that allow them to find and develop their own ideas. Play is the critical element that can provide the spark, the enjoyment, the real, total, personal involvement for children that an adult-centered art lesson lacks. I cannot overemphasize that at the heart of every art lesson for kids there must not be only inspiring art issues to consider, but fun, exciting forms of play, to keep the primary emphasis of the lesson where it belongs: on the children's own ideas, the unique, imaginative art ideas that only children can develop. Once this level of personal commitment and excitement has been reached, the teacher can also introduce students to the adult world of art, but should not begin with adult ideas and expect children to be interested in them. Children have to *feel* the personal value that art could have for them before they can develop great interest in pursuing it.

The teacher's presentation of art ideas, techniques, and materials will be dramatic, unusual, visually and imaginatively stimulating, and as playful as we can make it. Instead of a limited selection of materials, tools, and examples, the teacher will present a wealth of relevant materials, examples, and tools, encouraging students to experiment with the tools and materials and to play out their art ideas in a variety of forms, which may include storytelling, poetry, dance, or drama. The teacher's own performance will be as visually stimulating as it can be, amounting to a real "performance." In playing and experimenting with art materials and ideas in class, there will be many times when it will be valuable for the whole class to try out techniques, movements, and play ideas together, following the teacher's lead. The purpose of such communal activities, though, is always to feed back into the students' individual work and to inspire them to respond with their own ideas for play and experimentation—not to show them the one "right" way of doing it. I often puzzle my students by telling them *not* to do what I say—that although I've been drawing for years, I still don't know how to do it, and that I'm always learning about it—because there isn't any "right" way to draw, paint, sculpt, or make art. Identifying the kind of broad art and play ideas for lessons that stimulate children to discover their own art problems requires a new approach to lesson planning, which will be explored in detail in Chapter 4.

PLANNING AN ARTWORK AS AN IMPORTANT STEP IN THE ART PROCESS

All art making requires previsualization, planning, and the coming together within the artist of a great many different observations, images, emotions, and thoughts. This interior process of becoming aware of one's own observations and responses, keeping track of and recording them, thinking about them and identifying art ideas, selecting particular art ideas to work on and developing them over a period of time, and preparing to make particular artworks by experimenting with tools and materials is certainly just as much a part of the process of art making as the final physical manipulation of materials, yet this internal process tends to be neglected in art teaching. Obviously such planning is highly individual, involving uniquely personal observations, responses to experience, and art ideas, so if students are to learn how to make art on their own, art teaching has to help them experience this inner process that precedes physical art making. They have to find out that *their artworks begin with their own personal responses to experience; that art ideas precede art making and are just as important as physical artworks; and that planning a work is as exciting, and as important, as physically making it.* Children are bursting with all sorts of responses and observations that are potential art ideas, but they need the teacher's help in learning to be aware of, remember, and develop their ideas. This cannot be learned, of course, with production-line class management but only when learning activities are designed to stimulate personal investigation and show students how to plan artworks independently. In teaching children to plan their own artworks, we need to provide exciting and stimulating experiences; teach our students to record their responses and observations to such experiences in sketches, verbal notes, or other forms; and teach them to identify and develop their art ideas, presenting all this not just as a classroom or school activity but as a fundamental way of responding to experience that becomes part of their lives. Whether or not the planning or visualizing of art ideas results in a physical artifact, it is in itself a valuable way of understanding the world and oneself that can contribute enormously to children's individual development and self-confidence. In other words, we need to be less concerned, in art teaching, with having each child produce a certain number of art-works of certain types during the course, and more concerned with what kind of art learning is going on *inside* the child. I try to make my students just as proud of producing original art ideas (which have, of course, potential for future works) as they are of producing exciting physical works, and I celebrate such ideas just as much as I do the completion of a good work. As a teacher, I put as much stress on learning activities that promote inner exploration and experimental preliminary play with art materials as I do on the physical work that results in a "finished" artwork. For the artist, each artwork is only one in a sequence of works that leads from one work, and one idea, to the next, in a process that may continue through a whole series of works, and that ultimately continues throughout a lifetime. The quest itself is every bit as important and exciting as the various "endings" expressed in artworks, and each ending is capable of being a new beginning. For the artist, no work is ever necessarily "finished" (I have even given in to the temptation to alter drawings of mine that my friends had hung up in their homes when they made the mistake of leaving me alone in the room with them), but can always suggest a new way of approaching the art ideas expressed in it. The main thing we want students to take home with them after the art course is over is not a collection of artworks but a knowledge of how to set off on a personally satisfying adventure that may last them throughout their lives.

Planning for future art lessons also has to be shared with students, if they are to work independently. If students are to prepare for lessons, they have to know about them in advance. When the lesson itself is regarded as a work of art that the teacher is preparing, the students can participate in the planning process from another point of view: Besides planning their own works, they are participating in planning the lesson. Discussing ideas for future lessons with students gives the teacher a great opportunity to talk about how one gets art ideas and develops plans based on them, and the students will also get to see the "finished product" when the lesson is taught. Instead of having a lesson suddenly sprung on them on a subject they don't know about, if they have participated in planning the lesson they will have some familiarity with the subject and, often, quite a lot of curiosity about how the teacher's latest art experiment is going to turn out. (I discuss the planning of lessons in much more detail in Chapter 4.)

ENVIRONMENTAL SEARCH

I went to Sears one day to get the oil in my car changed. I came home with a wealth of ideas for art from the car maintenance department. I found a whole series of sculptures in the oil-change funnels they had on display. I bought one of each, not only so I could display them, but also to try painting with them. While I was in the store I also enjoyed the large selections of trolleys (flat boards with wheels on them, used by mechanics to slide under cars). What a fine view of the world you get while sliding on your back on this rolling contraption, I thought, imagining all the places I could slide around on as I or my students were sketching. A fundamental aspect of innovative teaching is to demonstrate to students the importance of constant searching—looking everywhere and considering all places as sources of art materials, tools, and ideas.

The environment can be viewed as the most complete gallery of art, displaying the works of artists (architects, designers, city planners, sculptors, etc.) as well as the art of nature and, in its complexity, the art built by chance juxtaposition or relationships among visual phenomena. Since everything in the environment moves and changes, it is an art that is constantly in transition. The environment is the experience and resource available to all and responded to by all artists.

The environment is also the largest art-supply store, containing all materials and tools that could possibly be used to make art. It was created by and is constantly being recreated by all kinds of techniques and processes. All of these need to be discovered, all of these can be borrowed and utilized by artists. The present array of materials, techniques, tools, or surfaces used by artists is only a small portion of what can be discovered in the larger environment.

In our teaching, we try to show students what art making is like for us, but often we fail to convey the real quality of the experience. Specific materials are introduced, but not the excitement of discovering a beautiful surface whose image we want to preserve; specific techniques are revealed, but not an understanding of how experiences were translated into the given art problem; specific concepts are handed down like formulas, but not the means of making a child's experiences of the environment more meaningful. How can we communicate to children the richness of the world around them, the joy of observation and discovery as it prods our imagination?

One way is to assign students to perform the search for ideas, materials, and tools to use in their art making as an essential part of preparing to make art. A second way is for teachers to share the environmental search that they perform for their own art making with their students. A third way is to provide a stimulating environment in the classroom, especially through experimental play with materials and through a visual approach to teaching. Let us examine all three approaches.

Artists do not simply use any available material; they aggressively search out the most interesting, unusual, or suitable material for working. Today, as we have noted earlier, many artists define the art process as the collecting of materials with interesting or beautiful surfaces and altering them by placing impressions or marks in them or on them. Contemporary artists look for art materials, tools, and ideas in a wide variety of places. For them, environmental search reaches beyond known and accepted art supplies, and thus beyond known and accepted themes or approaches to working. As openness to new art forms increased, materials from ice to ice cream have come to be used as art supplies. No one source can be called an art supplier, for any environmental form or substance can be used to make a work of art.

School art teaches just the opposite. Preliminary search is seldom the domain of the student. The selection of materials and art ideas is generally completed before the student enters the classroom; it is considered part of the teacher's responsibility in planning an effective lesson. Materials are given to children at their seats. The teacher suggests the proper art material to use, often without any discussion of the role of the material in shaping the work. Even teachers who prefer to emphasize the use of conventional materials and tools will find that having students make their own searches helps them to understand their art making. Searching for materials helps students to learn what they like and to discover the special characteristics of each material. Finding and using unusual or different materials helps the student to recognize their special properties and to be more aware of the qualities of even the most common art supplies. Each new material suggests its own possible uses and can also suggest art ideas or new processes. When students really know the materials they are working with, they can use them more effectively. Many of the objects collected (especially tools used by professionals in fields other than art) may suddenly be found to be useful as art tools that suggest new processes. The objects that are found do not, however, have to be used. They may simply inspire art ideas.

The search for materials and tools is, in general, also a search for art ideas. Searching through a variety of forms and objects develops the artist's ability to previsualize possibilities—that is, the uses, combinations, or alterations of materials—simply by seeing and feeling the material or form that is found. The search can help to formulate a new idea or expand an old one. Often the search makes an idea within the artist's mind more concrete, so that it undergoes a process of growth and change. Searching for materials is a way of planning an artwork through active experimentation and play.

Assigning students to collect materials requires advance preparation by both the teacher and the students. Through class lessons the teacher must define in advance a broad area within which students are to make their individual investigations and collect their materials.

The actual searching can be done both outside the classroom and within it. Much of the searching should be done outside of school in the student's ordinary environment—the home, the neighborhood, the shopping mall. In this way students learn that resources for art are all around them every day, and that when a visit to the ballpark, the video arcade, or the fast-food store is approached with a special spirit—with the idea of "using one's artistic vision"—ideas and materials for art are everywhere. They begin to understand that art does not come from some mysterious world that only the artist knows but from their own environment. They learn the thrill of looking at everything as a possibility for art. Although many people in the neighborhood travel to the same stores and cross the same streets, students will learn the difference between going as an ordinary pedestrian and going as an artist who is ready to perceive, observe, and explore his or her surroundings.

Shopping for art supplies is a valuable form of environmental search. Every store can be seen as a potential source of materials and tools for art. Students can learn to look at the fabric store, the building supply store, the paint or hardware store, the antique store, and the Salvation Army store as possible resources. In shopping, students need to learn to change from a functional to a creative way of seeing when approaching familiar places. For example, one can go to a supermarket to fill a shopping list or to study the packaging, labels, and color relationships exhibited by package and display designs. Materials and displays at the bakery, florist, or fast-food restaurant can suggest ideas for sculpture, new materials, surfaces, and tools.

Recently, I brought the brushes I paint with to share with my classes. We were all surprised that brushes can be found everywhere. The toothbrushes, hairbrushes, and nail brushes I paint with came from a drug store. In any supermarket, I am drawn to the "art-brush" selection, and I am always looking for scrub brushes, bottle brushes, or makeup brushes. At the janitorial supplier, I search for mops and brooms for my larger works. At large chain stores, I find interesting tub-cleaning and shoeshine brushes, lint brushes, and venetian blind brushes. In the kitchen store, in addition to the funnels, basting tube, and other tools, I have found my collection of feather brushes. At the sporting-goods store, my golf-ball cleaning brush was discovered. A variety of typewriter-, computer-, and photo-equipment-cleaning brushes are available for fine detail work. My most unusual brush is a motorized, revolving face-massage brush that creates swirling areas of paint.

The fast-food restaurant, which both children and artists frequent, has important collections of things that can be saved as art objects and art supplies. The paper goods—trays, place mats, and napkins—make fine soft surfaces to paint on. Painting tools abound, from the plastic utensils to the straws and the small squeeze packets of mustard and ketchup, which can be refilled with paint. There are sculpture ideas and materials in the signs, packaging, and food containers, in the paper hats worn by employees, and in the prizes given to children. The creatively shaped plastics, styrofoam, foil, and other exciting materials are all adaptable for art use. The boxes and shrink wraps can suggest three-dimensional canvases or sculptural forms. The carefully lighted foods offered at a salad bar have been sliced and diced as a sculptural act and are displayed as areas of color. The carefully arranged, well-lit foods at the salad bar and the stage-lit foods under the heat lamp at the serving counter suggest many ideas for painting, which deals with the display of color, the staging of lines, the arrangement of forms, the discovery of new surfaces, and interesting ways of applying color.

Ideas for drawing can be found in all sorts of stores, for many professions use drawing tools and techniques and a great many everyday life activities involve drawing. One can observe drawing in the post office, for example, in the wrapping of packages with string and tape. The tapes, strings, and dispensers can be viewed as drawing tools, as can the different stamping and marking tools used by the post office clerks. At the bakery, decorative drawings abound, and the pastry tubes and special spray-frosting tools that are used for cake decorating can be adapted for painting. A thorough and systematic exploration of different types of stores helps to extend the range of possibilities for art supplies, allowing young artists to look at everything and adapt from everywhere.

I stress shopping as a form of environmental search for several reasons. First, the design arts and commercial arts are subject to competition and the need to keep up with constantly changing fashions and styles. Because commercial designers use the latest technology and materials, their products often provide clues to the newest art ideas. For example, new package designs in which materials are molded to display the product can be great sources of innovative sculptural ideas. Shopping also helps us to be aware of ordinary, everyday objects that can be redesigned or transformed by artistic thought. Artists work both by taking *from* the environment objects of beauty that inspire their work and by taking the ordinary and redesigning it, giving back something beautiful *to* the environment. Shopping promotes both of these aspects of art making, helping us to keep in close touch with the environment.

By "shopping," I do not necessarily mean purchasing, which would be much too expensive for many students and teachers. "Creative browsing" is really what I have in mind—an imaginative search through the multitude of various forms, designs, and objects available in even the simplest hardware or discount store, with the idea of discovering how these things could be adapted for making art.

For students who are not brought up with regular visits to art museums, shopping for toys (assisted in many cases by television advertising) has provided some of their most intense visual experiences. This is therefore a good place to start for art teaching. Shopping also gives art teachers and students a common point of reference. It is the environment they share; both know it and can refer to it as a common resource when they exchange finds or show collections. Shopping provides a common language for classroom show-and-tell sessions, so that it is not necessary to acquire a special art language to access what one is looking at.

Shopping teaches students to find art ideas everywhere, not just in art-supply stores or in artworks. It teaches alertness to daily life and the need to try to find extraordinary things ignored by others and to visualize them in personal ways. Shopping, in other words, teaches observation and awareness skills, so that experiences can be recorded and responded to artistically.

When the shopping experience is reproduced in the classroom, so that students, for example, select materials from a "flea-market" display rather than having them handed to them, they learn the process of extensive looking and searching for the materials that will best express their ideas.

The need to constantly shop for school is good for teachers, too. Teachers often order supplies from catalogs for an entire year in advance. Catalog shopping does not provide the excitement of making new finds daily and, since the supplies are shipped, teachers cannot tell stories describing their personal searches and discoveries. The materials used are ordinary school supplies, and going through the catalog is not a process of discovery but a yearly chore. Instead of being concerned with buying supplies efficiently, we need to teach how to shop and observe by our own example.

Some specification or plan is often necessary for students. Shopping trips can range from an open exploration of everything in a specific store to a prescribed search for art elements, design ideas, or object categories in one or several stores. All trips are exploratory to a degree, and even when they have the most specific list, students need to be trained to expect detours and to be challenged by surprises. Students can enter a store with some preliminary ideas, sketches, or possibilities in mind and explore only what they came to see. They can decide in advance on a category, such as the labels and folders in a stationery store, or their task could be to find the most unusual, beautiful, simplest, or even the worst design. The excitement of search and discovery should be part of the experience, and teachers need to respect the individual findings of their students. Developing categories of objects gives them a basis for comparison and a taste in designed forms.

Students need to be taught that the most important aspect of art cannot be communicated. That holds true for making art or for experiencing it. Thus, all the experiences of a shopping trip cannot be predicted in advance or its value be completely evident to the shopper. During the shopping process, many ideas flow about, and their contribution to a richer visual environment is of great value in itself. Some of the ideas we may recall. Some we subconsciously store or discard. Suggesting general areas to look for, developing preliminary views, focusing on a specific problem, and explaining beforehand what is to be seen in a store may all help develop the confidence of the shoppers.

Shopping is an adventure; it should be anything but routine. We can enter a fabric store to look for a surface to paint on or sculpt with, and immediately see the store in a new light with a new purpose. With creative intention, students tend to look more carefully, willing to review a wider number of possibilities and to follow their instincts, taking detours to find what they want. The open and inventive frame of mind required in shopping is similar to that required in creating artwork. Like any other part of the art process, shopping requires a playful manipulation of objects and ideas, of creating possibilities in our minds and selecting and reacting to them.

INVESTIGATION OF MATERIALS

In order to get to know the materials found in an environmental search, students need to handle and discuss them. They need to have the opportunity to examine materials carefully, seeing how they tear, stick, and roll. In the discovery of how materials "work," new and creative statements can be made. The investigation also aims to expand and exhaust the category from which an object comes. Another objective is to discover and consider with what it can be combined. Dissimilarities among materials can also be noted. In using stickers, for example, students can see how these materials are different from standard drawing paper: They are smaller; available in sets, geometric multiples, or modules in large quantities; and peeled or stuck to surfaces. In other words, students should discover the appropriate technique for using a particular material and find the other materials it works best with. The matching or contrasting of one material with another is the artistic process of bringing together visual surfaces and forms into composition.

Another way to learn about the material is to think about what it suggests to its finder. Take a sticker, for instance. Students can say it looks like a stamp, a label on a jar, or a miniature movie screen. Each one of these ideas could suggest an artwork: a stamp design, a label, or a thousand stickers forming miniature screens to be projected on.

Finding out how different people mark different surfaces is an important part of the artistic search. Each profession, artistic or not, works with different movements and requires different tools and surfaces for leaving impressions and ideas. For instance, the simplest tool, the crayon, has a variety of uses: in a lumber yard to mark wood, in a supermarket to mark products, or in a butcher shop to mark meats. Further, each of these materials suggests that artists can use the same tool for marking different surfaces. Artists can also use different tools to mark the same surfaces.

Different design professions use different equipment, from the variety of curved rulers used in fashion design, to the T square of the architect, to the stencils of the industrial designer, including the vellums, grid sheets, and ruling pens that are all possible adaptations for personal creative statements. The frosted impressions of a cake decorator or the tools and impressions of a car-body-repair person, using materials such as lacquers and spray paint, also inspire new artistic possibilities. Design and art professions may be specialized in their processes, tools, and materials, yet the art student can borrow, restate, and mix in a personal way a variety of materials and surfaces. The tools, surfaces, or materials routinely used in one profession can be seen as symbolic or beautiful by another artist, who experiments with them and rediscovers them in a fresh way.

Each material and surface suggests possibilities and defines limitations. Thus, office supplies, developed for efficient recording, storage, and retrieval of information, have their own way of organizing, displaying, communicating, and storing ideas. Their scale and purpose are designed for efficient coding and decoding of handwritten or mechanical impressions. Designs are scaled to the printed line and coded for easy reading. By discussing the original intent of a material, students can develop new uses for it. The use of a paintbrush on a computer sheet is different from the mechanical impressions the surface was intended for. Bookkeeping sheets designed for tightly written columns to be marked on with a pointed tool can be filled in with woven rows of stamped colors or freely responded to with fluid paints from an oversized paintbrush. Students may develop an interest in the beauty of lined paper, in the ingenious folding of stationery pads, or in the marking devices used by accountants.

For the art student, the discovery of new materials must be accompanied by a relevant artistic response, for an exciting discovery should not simply be used to continue marking the same surface with the same attitude. Beyond their significance as surface and a new material resource, materials and processes of other professions need to be seen as a result of designing for a human task. Each new material has accessories that help to suggest how it can be attached, marked, sealed, and so forth. Hole punchers, staplers, and typewriters are the accessories of office materials. All may be thought of as the marking or drawing tools of the medium. Of course, knowing the intended use of a supply or found material should not restrict the use of it; students should feel a complete freedom to adapt their finds.

Each field of human endeavor has unique means of storing, retrieving, and displaying its marks of information. In using the surfaces, tools, and processes of another field, the artist is creatively responding to them. The response to the material may be a logical extension of the original materials, for some found forms are beautiful and need only to be discovered, not redesigned. The surfaces one finds in different stores are not without purpose but are the result of designers' clear intention to accomplish specific functions with specific tools and techniques of imprinting. The artistic response to a material may range widely from its intended use. The student shopper needs to recognize the material's intent but feel free to adapt it to his or her own needs. In accepting, say, a telephone answering pad as a stage for building art,

Artist's sketchbook: Observations
of movements during public school recess.

the student learns to declare that as an artist he or she is free to make impressions on all surfaces with all kinds of materials and tools. It is important for a contemporary artist to feel this freedom.

SHOW AND TELL:
SHARING EVERYONE'S FINDS

The familiar show-and-tell session is an excellent device to use, at all age levels, to display and discuss collections and the finds made during environmental search and to discuss the ideas they have suggested. These do not have to be formally organized sessions in which everyone is expected to give a little speech describing what he or she has brought. They can be informal times for sharing and discussing everyone's latest finds, perhaps in relation to a future lesson that is being planned and for which students are making searches and gathering ideas. Students enjoy seeing each other's finds, which are often surprises to everyone. They also get ideas from them for their own searches and artworks, and one person's unusual discovery may inspire others to find something even more outrageous. Teachers too can display their latest discoveries or their favorite collections and discuss how they have led to artworks, helping students to learn how to use their finds. Show and tell provides a natural opportunity for discussing art ideas. By openly welcoming all finds to the art class, showing how they reflect each student's individual interests, and by talking with students about methods of environmental search and possibilities for building from their finds to new ideas and works, we help students to gain confidence in their own ability to get and develop art ideas. Students, by observing how others (including the teacher) make finds and react to them, and how they plan, learn about the planning process and are able to observe each other's progress. In this way, when a student's ideas or works are seen again at a later stage of development, perhaps in an exhibit or some other student presentation, everyone is familiar with the earlier stages of the project and knows something about how it grew and developed. Works do not just appear from nowhere in one class session; in many cases students have contributed to each other's art with perceptive comments or suggestions that are reflected in the finished work, and the experience of art making has been a shared, rather than a lonely, separate, and competitive, experience. (In Chapter 5, I discuss the value of talking about finished artworks as a way of evaluating them.)

SKETCHBOOKS

Although most visual artists, and many other creative people (such as scientists, writers, mathematicians, and choreographers), keep sketchbooks or notebooks to record their observations and plan their works, sketchbooks seldom receive much emphasis in art class. I have found, through experience, that having students keep sketchbooks, idea books, or some other form of personal record and planning book is essential to art teaching: It is one of the best ways to help students learn to work independently and to understand the source of artworks and of art ideas. Being asked to record their observations, thoughts, and visions helps children to realize that the artworks they make come from inside themselves, and that their own ideas are valuable and worthwhile exploring in depth and at length, in a variety of ways.

The type of record book can be varied and personalized to meet the needs of the particular student. Notes can be made in the form of sketches, drawings, or printings, or can consist of photographs, personal writings, diary entries, or any other item that can serve as a record so that the sketchbook may really be more of a scrapbook or diary. The name and the purpose of the sketchbook can vary. It can be called a "doodlebook," an "idea file," or a planning kit, with each name reflecting a different approach to its use. The sketchbook can be specialized, working out a specific project, theme, or concept, or it can explore the environment randomly. Students can even have several sketchbooks—a night-table sketchbook, a day travel book, and a special-occasion book, for instance.

Teachers should not assign or distribute the same type of book to all students. If students are to gather unique responses through sketching, personal variation in sketchbook format should be encouraged, so that students feel the books are really theirs. The sketchbook may have a beautiful cover with a ribbon around it, or it may be an informal scrapbook with clippings. The student's choice of sketchbook reflects his or her personal working style. Some students may work best on high-quality drawing paper. Others may want a smaller and more informal format such as a note pad or address book. Some may want an intimate book containing lots of paper, so that there will be greater opportunity for freely generating ideas. Others may prefer fewer working papers, because they are better able to internally visualize their works and need fewer visual notes to move from stage to stage. Unusual stationery, a mechanical engineer's notebook, music sheets, or receipt pads can all be used as sketchbooks. Some students may want to use a box or folder to compile individual sheets whose order can be altered freely to form different patterns. Others may want a spiral book with perforated paper for easy tearing. Sketches can even be kept in secret places. A conscious choice of format promotes the individuality of response that will ultimately dictate the look of the works planned from the sketches.

Since the sketchbook is designed to record personal, spontaneous responses to experience, students should be encouraged to take notes anytime and all the time. It is important that the sketchbook be available whenever the child needs it. Children should be urged to carry a sketchbook or camera at all times, so that they can take notes whenever inspiration strikes. Such moments are unpredictable and need to be caught, even after a shower or a bad dream, so students should also be encouraged to use whatever surface is convenient for their note taking. Ideas scribbled on a crossword puzzle in a newspaper or on a vitamin-jar label at breakfast can later be collected and put into an idea file. A plastic notebook may be used for recording bathing experiences, a sketchbook for the breakfast table or one for recording dreams may be kept under one's pillow.

Students also need to learn, however, that many artists have favorite places that they find personally inspiring, and that each of us must discover the special circumstances that make our ideas flow. Among artists there are the late-nighters and those who work best in the early morning light, those who prefer the times of day that are extraordinarily quiet, and those who find that changes in nature suggest changes, and hence ideas, in them. We can suggest that they try to work at different times of day, for example, watching the sun come up or taking a walk as it goes down.

Sketchbooks have great value in helping students learn how art ideas are generated and developed. First, the need to record their experiences teaches them how to look at and understand the environment. In sketching or otherwise recording their feelings and experiences while they are fresh, they become immersed in the environment. At the same time, they are responding to it from a personal perspective, for sketches can focus not only on the outer world but also on one's innermost thoughts. A sketchbook gives young artists a place to dare the impossible. Here they feel free to test their ideas, knowing that the results will not be evaluated, as they explore the endless possibilities the sketchbook format can provide. Here they can record their dreams and fantasies without being made fun of. While the adult artist can retreat to a studio for such experimentation, often only the sketchbook can afford the young artist the privacy needed to create.

Young artists need to be free to "talk" to themselves on paper, something they should not be ashamed of. Indeed, they should be encouraged to take their creative intuitions seriously and to feel pride in their own ideas. Sketchbooks can help them recognize that we all have ideas that are of value. Furthermore, the diversity of sketchbook material shows them that they have many ideas of value to offer. Even sketchbooks that are also scrapbooks and include the sketches and ideas of well-known artists can be useful, for young artists may be encouraged by seeing their ideas side-by-side with those of Paul Klee or Piet Mondrian.

A sketchbook not only helps students plan finished works but also helps them approach these works more confidently. This is especially important in the classroom, for students feel the pressure to produce "acceptable" works keenly. The sketchbook helps them maintain the sense of the original idea. They can use it to keep the finished work on track, to renew their inspiration as they work away from it. Intentions or ideas that may get lost in the finished work are saved in the sketchbook.

Sketching fixes experiences deeply in the mind. As more and more impressions are recorded, students find it easier to organize their responses to the environment and to search out the meaning of their experiences. With each new entry the sketchbook will become more comfortable to use, freer in its drawing, and more self-confident in its markings. Freedom in visualizing becomes so easy that it is almost as if the students were talking to themselves, keeping a diary in pictures. The results are the richest clues available, for both student and teacher, to the individual artistic perceptions of each student.

The sketchbook is especially useful in helping the art teacher penetrate a child's personality and ideas. Although initially it is a monologue, a healthy communication through which children come to know themselves, ultimately it can become a sort of dialogue with the outside world. The art teacher can take advantage of this direct means of communication with the young artist to encourage his or her development. When sketchbooks are shared with the teacher, the teacher can guide each child's efforts from the creation of an initial sketch to the completion of finished works.

Children will soon learn that keeping a sketchbook is not just an idle pastime but a way of life. This realization is critical, for it allows them to develop as artists through independent efforts to guide the course of their work. Thus, for children the sketchbook begins by enhancing the teaching process and ends as a means of building away from the teacher and discovering their own artistic concerns. The earlier the child breaks away from the teacher's guidance the fresher and more wonderful these ideas will be.

Through sketching, students develop a capacity for independent investigation and judgment. When given the freedom to do what they want, students must face the question, "What do I want to do?" They must learn to decide for themselves how and when to take notes, how to sort and file them, how to pursue them, and when to return to sketches. They must learn to sort through numerous pages of ideas, selecting what is best. Soon they are able to set boundaries for themselves while keeping their options open. As they assess finished works by comparing them with initial sketches and plan from one artwork to the next, they learn to set the direction of their work for themselves.

Through sketching, students learn that art making is a series of problem-solving tasks. Notations in sketchbooks represent artistic queries that are answered through sketching. As students look back at sketches and forward to the plans based on them, they can consider many alternatives, both simple and complex. They learn to see solutions to the visual problems presented by these alternatives, and their responses to these problems are not hasty but considered and fully developed. Although they begin by making notes on anything of interest, they learn to use their sketchbooks to investigate specific problems in an orderly and persistent fashion. With a sketchbook, then, the art-making process becomes deliberate. Sketches are the closest thing possible to the artist's vision unaltered by subsequent judgments, and with these sketches on hand, students keep the art idea in focus as they work. They do not enter into the art-making process without purpose or thought.

Once the work is completed, it may not be a success. Sketchbooks help the young artist deal with the feelings of frustration and failure that are a part of all art making. Often the sketchbook offers an unexpected solution to an ailing work of art. If not, students can still return to it to get ideas for new works, and its clean pages offer the opportunity for a fresh start.

Sketchbook material is often less exciting in the quality of its drawing than in its ability to display the thought process, for in making their notes, children are more concerned with conveying a message than with perfecting the manner in which it is conveyed, and their ideas are often far ahead of their abilities. In time, students will polish their skills and learn to specify what the finished work will look like. But even if they cannot always carry out these specifications to perfection, they can experience the excitement of the imagination's leaping from a simple sketch to the possibilities beyond it.

The sketchbook teaches students discipline, since they must make steady contributions to it if they are ever to achieve a finished work. It also helps them to keep track of how their works are progressing. By looking through the sketchbook with the student, the teacher can also observe the progress. The teacher can assess the student's commitment to an idea simply by noting the number of entries (although of course teachers should not impose quotas, since no outsider can know how many sketches a work may require).

To get students started with their sketchbooks, teachers can share their own notebooks with students, explaining how they use them. Teachers can also show students the sketchbooks of various artists and of others who use notations in their work, pointing out the personal styles of different individuals and the unique notation system of each profession, and helping them trace the development of an idea through a series of trials and errors that help clarify the individual's intentions.

Warming up by doodling quick sketches of ideas derived from observation or free association is a good way to begin the process of recording. Students can then go on to interpret these intuitive expressions, even adding labels or other written materials if they wish. To inspire a series of works, teachers should make assignments that appeal to students' varied interests and aspirations. For example, teachers can assign the use of a sketchbook for special times and places. Special sketch trips to a parade, circus, or ballet may be taken and the book dedicated to the event. In group discussions with students, exercises may be suggested to teach them to serialize an idea, taking a single sketch of an idea and following it through successive stages of investigation. Students can benefit from exercises that teach them how to translate sketchbook material into finished works. Specifying the finished product, designating the steps that will be taken to elaborate a sketch, previsualizing how a sketch will look in another medium or scale, and creating models and blueprints that go beyond the sketchbook format are examples of such exercises. Once students have completed these exercises, they can then be asked to plan works in a sequence. This will give them a sense of continuity and purpose.

Once inspired by exercises to work on their own, students will want to discuss their sketchbook finds. They should be given the opportunity to discuss their ideas both with peers and with teachers whenever they feel that audience reaction would be helpful. The teacher's comments are particularly useful at this point. He or she can help to free up their ideas by pointing out unconventional as well as conventional associations among the possibilities spread out on the sketchbook page; help students plan alternatives, enlargements, or transformations of their ideas; and by showing respect for unusual ideas, both reward and inspire creativity. The teacher's role is to help guide the work from initial sketch to finished product. Eventually students will have enough confidence to initiate their own assignments and plan their own works.

Since students will use sketchbooks outside of school as well as in the classroom, parental support is necessary if sketchbooks are to become a regular part of the students' routine. Parents must be asked to make room for the sketching process at home and to help students perceive it as a useful and important activity. They can do so by making available the time and space for the recording of notations and, whenever possible, by planning events such as museum visits that contribute interesting materials to the sketching process. Parents can serve as supportive audiences, discussing with their children ideas that have been recorded in the notebook. They should learn to enjoy their children's unique sketches and should gently encourage them to produce more. By carefully watching what their children are attracted to when they work and what directions and interests they express, parents can gain useful insights into their children that can be shared with the teacher.

EXPERIMENTATION

As suggested by this chapter, experimentation is one of the most important parts of art making. Making a work of art is not a linear process in which the artist starts with an idea, chooses materials, tools, and techniques, and makes the work in a single attempt. The "steps" don't always occur in this order; often, for example, a particular material one has gotten interested in, or an artwork one is making, suggests an idea for another work. Although an experienced artist may sometimes go directly from initial idea to finished artwork, more often the original idea changes as it is being worked on, and some of the best new ideas are discovered while the original idea is being carried out. Each artwork is a culmination or summary of the numerous visions and ideas generated during the art making—most of which could not have been predicted by anyone, even by the artist, in advance. It is only by looking at the finished work later and remembering the sequence of changing ideas one had about the work as it developed

that one can see (although probably not fully remember or understand) how the crucial decisions were made and when they occurred.
Artists know that it is important to take the time to experiment, even
when other urgent considerations (such as the desire to show a picture)
press them to hurry.

Art teachers know the importance of experimentation, but in
practice we tend to give priority to other things. We often plan lessons
that require each student to finish an artwork within one class period.
Therefore the beginning of class must be used for giving instructions;
the end is for cleanup; the middle is mostly for constructing the
artwork, in accordance with the instructions. Very little time is left for
experimentation. Frequently, children are expected to start making
the project as soon as the teacher has given the instructions, with no
opportunity to practice or to become familiar with the materials and
tools. Sometimes students are given only one sheet of "good" art paper
for a drawing or painting lesson and are told that if that sheet is ruined,
no more will be available: In other words, they have to get it right the
first time or fail entirely. Under such pressure, even experienced artists
might lose their self-confidence and spontaneity.

The design and pacing of an art lesson must make it clear to
students that finishing the work is not the only or even the most
important goal—that experimenting and learning *while* one is making
it, acquiring knowledge about art or about oneself as an artist that will
carry over to the next, work and the next, are just as important, and
just as satisfying.

TIME MANAGEMENT

The limited time made available for art classes in the school
curriculum is, of course, a serious obstacle. How can we give children
time to experiment if we meet with them only occasionally? Like the
other limitations we face, this one too can be approached as a challenge. We can take advantage of the fact that many of the preparations
for art making, such as environmental search, can be performed just as
well or better outside of class than in, and, since we want children to
be working independently anyway, such homework is a good way of
teaching them to prepare for art making on their own. Also, our goal of
having students work independently implies that they will not be
doing uniform projects that must all begin and end at the same time.
We can help students plan long-term projects that will extend over
several class periods, leaving ample time for experimentation. Learn-

ing to manage one's time is part of being an artist. Artists never have enough time for all that they would like to do, no matter how much time is available, so it is good for students to have to learn to manage their time for art, both within school and in the rest of their daily lives. Students need to understand that the most difficult problem for any artist is to find the necessary time to work. All schools have strict time schedules, as do jobs that students may do after school. In contrast, artists work all the time. They work at different speeds and spend different amounts of time on different aspects of their work. While some artists spend months on a painting (I myself spend months in contemplation), preparing for the physical act may take only a few seconds. Art teaching at every level needs to show teachers and students how artists stretch time, make time, and listen to their inner sense of time in adjusting their lives and work. All art learning, in a sense, needs "time management" to become familiar with how slow or fast we work. In other words, whatever limited school time is available, it should be considered as only part of the students' time spent on art, meant to inspire observation, collecting, note taking, and other important art tasks performed outside of the class time. In essence, students are learning how art time has to be built into one's daily life.

3

Creating a Classroom Environment Favorable to Artistic Learning

Young children, when they make art, find great pleasure in scribbling, actively enjoying the materials and the movements they are making, and the recording of these movements on a surface. The adult artist experiences similar satisfaction in feeling a brush bounce over a span of canvas or watching the paint soak into it. Young children, in their scribbling, invent a variety of patterns and greatly enjoy their playful yet serious experimentation. The "dance" of the hand results in a wide variety of lines and movements on the surface. The children feel the material and even hear the contact with it. They are excited about the sensations of the work and even by the smell of the media.

Before they go to school, young children can express their feelings and ideas in their artworks, just as they can relate experiences and emotions in their play. They make few distinctions between the way they experience the world verbally or sensorially. Their actions combine the emotional and the intuitive, as well as the logical and the rational. They create images of art and discuss them freely, without separating the joy involved in these experiments from what is regarded as work. Self-generated knowledge is not distinct for the child; it is just as valuable as knowledge received from teachers.

In school, verbal expression—reading and writing—receives great emphasis. Drawing is encouraged only on special occasions, usually during designated art periods. Ideas are generally expressed and discussed in words. Drawings—which are natural forms of note taking, planning, and expressing ideas—are discontinued at an early age by many children. Only grafitti remain as a vestige of free, childlike self-expression. There are few opportunities in school to exercise the extensive visual knowledge that children have acquired through exposure to

47

*Plastic hangings inspired
by children's costume designs.*

media. Teaching is designed to appeal to the intellect and is not conceived of or presented visually to inspire the senses.

An instrument such as a ballpoint pen could be used for creative scribbling as well as for writing, but in school, after countless penmanship exercises, the pen is used as a mechanical device rather than a creative tool. Penmanship encourages control, uniformity of output, and clarity, but lines that before freely danced on the page after penmanship exercises become timid and uninventive. Before conventional training, the drawn line encompasses message, emotion, and line quality. After such training this line becomes merely routine duplication of predetermined symbols.

The emphasis placed on reading skills does not prepare the child well for seeing. At school, the child learns to consult visual references only if they are presented as part of a story or accompanied by a subtitle. The visual is often regarded merely as an aid to or illustration of the verbal: Pictures are used to illustrate reports or to make other assignments more palatable. Outside of art class, visual information is seldom used independently of stories of explanatory text.

Since school instruction is planned to appeal to the intellect rather than to the senses or emotions, children begin to distrust the senses as a basis of discovery and communication. School learning thus prepares the child poorly for artistic expression, which requires the integration of sensory, emotional, and intellectual responses to experience.

Art education has to return to the child's natural style of sensory learning in play and base its approach on the child's creative beginnings. Painting and drawing should be extensions of the child's initial "messings" with materials, the child's original pleasure in making free scribblings, experimental lines, unregimented colors, and in experiencing materials. Such drawing or painting play is not far removed from the spirit of the drips of Jackson Pollock, the stains of Helen Frankenthaler, and the sprayings of Jules Olitsky. Architectural studies with block playing may extend into other areas of balancing forms, overcoming gravity, matching modular units. Continued investigations of sandbox situations may uncover free building forms in plastic, or clay, while playing house may lead to the creation of new interiors.

I described in the preface how, as a young teacher, I had to find nonverbal ways of communicating with my students because they did not speak English. Later, in working with English-speaking children, I found that these nonverbal techniques were still very effective and they felt more comfortable to me, as an artist, than lecturing. Gradually teaching became more a matter of showing a color, holding an interesting object, exploring the possibilities of balance with interesting shapes in front of a class, rather than talking about (and perhaps illustrating) them. As time passed, I began to feel that my objects, my alterations of the environment, the beautiful things I placed before the class, spoke more eloquently than I would have. I began to shift my emphasis from designing visual presentations that illustrated my speaking to planning full-fledged visual presentations that might perhaps be supplemented by language. When I was talking about, say, warm colors, I became more concerned with what I wore, or the surface I walked over, or the light in the room, than with some precise formula for describing them. I considered the art sessions a means of visually inspiring my students; of showing, rather than telling; of demonstrating a variety of possibilities; of presenting beautiful experiences in concrete visual terms.

After years of experience, I have found it so valuable to rely on the special nature of art in teaching that I now encourage the university students in my art education classes to plan their art lessons as pieces of visual communication, specifically instructing them to make believe that their students do not speak English. Art lessons can be designed as visual messages; the instructor does not merely talk about art but shows or performs it, inviting others to experience the art concept that is the focus of the lesson.

A good art lesson is a design for creating in the classroom an environment that challenges children to make art. Such an environment, if it is to involve children fully, must provide a multisensory experience that calls forth physical, emotional, and imaginative responses. The strategies for achieving such an environment focus especially on visual presentations; creative play experiences; and use of art forms such as drama, dance, music, and literature—art forms that synthesize intellectual knowledge with sensory and emotional experience.

More specifically, the basic elements that must be considered in creating an environment in the classroom favorable to art are:

1. *Material design*: Selecting a wide variety of materials, tools, and surfaces for art work and presenting them in unusual, visually interesting ways.
2. *Display*: Selecting beautiful or interesting forms, objects, and works of art to exhibit to students and displaying them in imaginative ways.
3. *Classroom design*: Creative use of the shape, space, and furnishings of the classroom to make a visual statement.

4. *Play*: Involving children in creative play experiences that lead to unexpected events, to unusual visual experiences, and to experimentation in art making.
5. *Performance*: Presenting teaching as a performance, and the teacher's presentation of the entire lesson as a coordinated performance—a work of art. The "performance" in this broader sense includes the material design, displays, classroom design, and creative play, and may also make use of art forms such as drama, dance, music, literature, poetry.

In planning such an art lesson, we need to broaden the scope of our thinking. In contrast to a lecture, an art lesson can—indeed, should—involve a wide variety of things to see and styles of presentation. Through the look and feel of the art materials, the placement of furniture, even the teacher's manner of dress, the art idea can be made visible. It is as if these things were canvases for painting or a sculptor's clay. Instead of a lecture based on standardized lesson plans that tell the teacher what to say, what to write on the board, and what assignments to make, the lesson is an exciting experience for the students. It is special and different—a break from the routines of the school day. Everything in the lesson is designed to show students, or to let them discover—rather than *telling* them—how artists approach their work and what they look for. The multisensory approach, the use of play experiences, and the use of other art forms are designed to involve students in a holistic experience, integrating sensory, physical, emotional, imaginative, and intellectual elements. By mainly circumventing the usual verbal and intellectual forms of communication used in school, we surprise children into learning with pleasure.

Let us now look at each of the major elements of such a classroom experience in turn, beginning with the presentation of materials.

MATERIAL DESIGN

Contemporary artists, we noted earlier, regarded art materials not simply as the raw materials for art but as basic elements of the works, deserving attention and study in their own right. The qualities of individual materials suggest how they may be used. By exposing students to a wide range of materials, surfaces, and tools to use for art making, we encourage them to consider art media and processes in terms of their broadest definitions, before attempting to master the skills required for limited techniques—to think of printing, for example, as taking impressions *of* any sort of object *with* any sort of object, rather than as potato or woodblock printing.

Each kind of surface suggests a unique set of techniques and processes, and some provide greater opportunities for exploring a particular concept than do others. All sorts of different surfaces can be used for art—anything from styrofoam and plastics to rocks or sand—and the qualities of the surface will affect the kind of artwork that can be made from it. Children need to learn that any environmental surface can be used for an artwork, but not indiscriminately—that evaluating the qualities of a surface and (frequently.) preparing a surface is part of making a work of art. They need to learn to observe and investigate the colors and textures of all sorts of two- and three-dimensional surfaces; their feel; dense/open, supported/flexible, organized/random, whether they are hard or soft; rough, textured, or smooth; easy to inscribe or impenetrable; porous or impervious to liquids—and then to observe how different surfaces respond when they are changed by the addition of other materials and worked with various tools. A surface should never be approached as a given: Students need to know that even the ordinary school paper often used for art has particular qualities—color, texture, shape, porosity—that affect the work.

By making a wide variety of tools available to children, rather than limiting them to the traditional tools used for art making, we can help them to understand that artists constantly invent new tools and that the selection of a tool is one of the important choices that an artist makes. The kind of marks that each tool makes is unique, and so is its fine responsiveness to variations in movement and pressure. Each tool works better on some surfaces than on others, and each requires a different kind of handling. Some are more mechanical, others can respond to the artist's playfulness. Tools may be selected according to how they are held, how they fit the hand, the types of movement they require—whether they are pressed, pulled, pushed, or grasped. Each quality creates different impressions and responses.

By making environmental search part of the art lesson, we have already made it clear to students that the artist goes to the environment to find materials, surfaces, and tools; that there is an enormous variety to choose from; and that the choice is made by the artist. Since we are teaching children to become their own suppliers, they will be bringing many items to school that can be used for lessons. In addition to encouraging them to make specific collections, we can make a specific place for their finds in the classroom by keeping a large open container labeled "Surprising Finds" constantly available, as well as formal display shelves. As students learn that all environmental sources provide materials for art, they will begin to bring in items not only from their shopping trips but from other sources, such as their parents' work equipment or things salvaged from home remodeling jobs by plumbers, electricians, roofers, or carpenters—pieces of materials, sample books, leftover materials. The show-and-tell occasions at the beginning of a period, in which students present their finds and discuss their ideas for using them, provide a ready-made opportunity for displaying and examining materials. Such sessions always contain the element of surprise—for neither teacher nor students know exactly what each child will come up with. Some especially exciting finds included a salesman's case of old vacuum cleaner bags and brushes, an old school anatomy chart, a mask of dyed feathers. How much more exciting and dramatic it is to be introduced to art materials in this way than to simply have the teacher hand them out or to have children find familiar materials and tools already in place on their desks! The children's curiosity about each other's finds provides a natural occasion for discussing their plans for their artworks, and the teacher can, by nonjudgmental comments and questioning, suggest possible techniques and other things to consider in planning the artworks.

By defining the areas for environmental search in advance, the teacher is assured that most of the finds will be relevant to the lesson. Naturally, on many occasions, the teacher will also want to provide a particular selection of materials, surfaces, and tools for children to work with in class, focused on the broad lesson idea. When materials are presented for children to find when they enter the classroom, the placement and display should be designed to pique their curiosity and invite them to handle and investigate the materials. Cleverly designed material displays not only communicate specific art ideas but help to convert a generally sterile classroom environment into an arena of forms, colors, and patterns. Any classroom surface can be used for displays—things can be attached to or hung from the wall and ceiling in a variety of patterns. Floors can be used as a modular display area for blocks, marbles, or plastic worms or a place to explore different surfaces made from pieces of carpet or tiles, to make patterns in sand or water. On the walls, hooks and hangers can be arranged so that rolls of paper or long pieces of wallpaper hang down, or insulation materials or sticks can be leaned up against the walls. Windows can be used for light boxes, see-through displays, or displays viewed through peep holes. Mirrors, springs, streamers, and hanging inflatables can be hung from ceilings. The display can be laid out on the floor or in a special area of the room defined by a hand-painted sheet of plastic on which materials are presented as different-sized packages for students to open. Some things, though, can be hidden in the closet or under the teacher's desk, to be discovered as surprises. Some can be held back to be presented later in the period. Some can be presented as a flea market for individual browsing. Other materials can be designed to be presented in stages.

Just as individual materials indicated their own uses, so do combinations of materials presented together, since artworks are often made of material combinations. The particular materials placed in proximity in the room or simply presented together in the same lesson can suggest ideas for artworks without a word being said: White folders and shiny white masking tape, plastic cases for film slides and Day-Glo stickers, white carpet samples and food colors, ceiling tiles and black inks, circular sanding disks and metallic nail polishes, tea bags and white blotter sheets, and so forth. A standard-sized sheet of white paper with a 2B pencil, for example, suggests traditional art supplies and experiences, while a plastic shopping bag with Day-Glo markers suggests a different attitude toward supplies and art. A single sheet of paper with black graphite, black Conte crayon, and black charcoal suggests a certain set of explorations, while the addition of a box of tissues, erasers, and cotton balls suggests another direction of rubbing, shading, and smearing. Combinations of materials and tools can suggest experimental processes: Examples might include sponges or funnels placed next to containers full of paint, white plastic pipes with black markers, typewriter ribbons next to tracing wheels, furniture casters with finger paints, plastic blind slats and black shoe polish, hair blower with sheets of plastic, and so forth.

Placing materials and tools in different parts of the room and in different relationships to the room's surfaces and spaces will also help to suggest wordlessly various ways of working and, sometimes, sculptural ideas. Paper, for example, can be laid on the floor; taped over the entire top of a table, between tables; hung over a table or wrapping it; hung in a roll from the ceiling or a wall. A chair can be used as an easel, with the paper draped around it, over its seat, or on its back. Things can be placed in a large, open area or in a small, cramped space where the movements used for working must be limited—in a small tent, for example. The size of the surface can be as large as a wall or minuscule, such as the size of a fingernail, an artwork that would be viewed with a magnifying glass. Things can be deliberately placed next to the window, so that the view, light, shadows, and sounds may influence the work. Placing things on stairs or steps can indicate the sequence in which materials are to be approached.

Here are some examples of material designs. If you were a student, what would the following displays of materials and tools suggest to you?

- A table set with white paper tablecloth with matching place mats and napkins. Trays of black ink are placed about the plate in each setting.
- Trash cans gift-wrapped in soft, white rice paper. Long sticks with cotton tips are placed inside.
- Bright plastic lunch boxes covered with self sticking note papers and stickers. Drawing tools are inside.
- White paper lab coat worn by the teacher. Big, colored chalks are exposed from its pockets.
- Adding machine tapes rolled out in hallway. Bright red tool boxes are placed at intersections where the tapes meet.
- Open umbrellas are placed on the floor covered with white fabric. Tubs of paint and sponges are under each umbrella.

In addition to the visual pleasure that they offer in their own right, material displays are designed to set the stage for experimental play with art materials. (For further discussion, see the section entitled "Play" later in this chapter.)

DISPLAY

Art objects and works of art (or reproductions) on display are used to some degree in all art classes but often more as illustrations for a lecture than as visual statements in their own right. In displaying things, we try to show students a variety of objects (natural or manufactured) and works of art that illustrate the lesson idea, in as dramatic a way as we can. Visual examples should not merely express both the play idea and the art idea but should be the best—the most beautiful and interesting—examples we can find. Since we cannot always take children to a museum or to the outside world, we need to bring the best of the environment and the art world to them in the classroom.

The clarity of the examples illustrating the art idea is as important as their beauty. The presentation can focus on a single image, a category of images, or a wide variety of possibilities regarding a given medium, skill, or style. We can contrast art and environmental examples, the works of different artists, the works of the same artist at different periods, or the same subject handled in different media. In selecting objects to exhibit, we need to consider a whole range of possibilities: a crushed metal can, a fine sheet of handmade paper, a scouring brush with an unusual handle, a motorcycle toy, live animals, the spring mechanism of an old toy. By illustrating the far-reaching possibilities of the concept, the wide and complex range of examples that can embody it, the presentation teaches the students about the search for ideas. For many art ideas, however, a single beautiful object is sufficient. To show students "significant forms," I have used objects such as baskets, to explore the rhythmic surface patterns made by sculptors; antique painted cast-iron doorstops, as examples of folk sculpture; pitchers, as examples of form invention and functional design; and toy cranes, to illustrate the idea of movable sculpture. I also show students my collections of everyday objects, both antique and new: keys, marbles, scales, and buttons. Each collection of simple objects stimulates imaginative redesign, such as keys for opening a spaceship or a dungeon, or buttons for a giant: These can also inspire forms, colors, and textures. Collections of natural objects such as shells, antlers, and rocks inspire many ideas. Students are also fascinated by personal examples—the instructor's ties or eyeglasses, or the untying of a student's shoelaces to illustrate the concept of line.

The method used to show examples is important. We tend to hold things up quickly and to use them not for enjoyment or inspiration but to make a specific point. Instead, objects need to be displayed with showmanship, sequenced in meaningful and interesting order. Some objects encourage student examination; others are held up to be observed. To draw the audience into perception, the magician's touch is needed so that students see the teacher circling with objects, holding them fondly, examining them closely, and playing with them publicly. A "playful hand" is needed: We can try things on, manipulate them in different ways, juggle them, hold them up to the light, and view them close up, upside down, and from afar. One especially useful technique is to package display objects in advance and plan to unwrap them before the class. Children are always very curious to see what is in the packages and pay close attention as the things are unwrapped.

The sequence in which exhibits are shown is especially important in maintaining student interest. One can, for example, start with familiar, concrete things (such as toys) and progress to others that are more abstract or less familiar (perhaps from an earlier historical period or a different culture). Objects can be sequenced in order of size, color, or other design features, and the display becomes an occasion for comparing them and discussing their similarities and differences.

Sharing a collection of objects with students helps children to see how artists discover related forms in the environment and how they redesign and alter what they see. Collecting comes naturally to younger children, and they often have interesting collections in their pockets. A collection is, by definition, a category of objects, and we can easily demonstrate the various contrasts within the collection, pointing out differences in shape and material, in style and in culture: A Halloween mask from K–Mart can be compared with the celebration mask of an African tribe. Sharing a collection allows us to talk about the objects' history and their relationship to other objects and to art work.

Any sort of collection that teachers themselves find interesting can be used. Here is a list of a few of my personal collections that I enjoy using:

Bags: shopping bags, antique beaded bags, old school bags

Books: children's pop-up books, illustrated books from different countries, old comic books, illustrated mystery novels

Buttons: antique brass buttons, hand-painted buttons, salesman's sample books

Catalogs: Old Sears and Roebuck catalogues, major toy stores, camping equipment, parachute and fashion catalogs

Charts: old dental charts, anatomy charts, old blueprints and maps

Children's clothing: animal gloves, superhero slippers, silk-screened T-shirts, unusual hats

Costumes: historic clothing items, unusual jewelry, head dressings, ties, paper and plastic garments

Covers: folk art tablecloths, quilts, Asian rugs, designer linen, siding and shingle samples

Dolls: old Barbie dolls, voodoo dolls, cutout paper dolls, teddy bears, ceramic female-head planters

Dishes: Fiesta dishes, Russel Wright dinnerware, paper dishes, Italian plastic dishes, Depression glass

Extenders of vision: magnifying glasses, binoculars, microscopes, telescopes, camera lenses, plastic magnifying sheets, kaleidoscopes

Edibles: lollipops, candy in see-through bags, boxes of assorted chocolates, ice cream charts, food display, place mats, sandwich greeting cards, restaurant menus

Gloves: hunting, surgical, work, old baseball, children's, kitchen mitts

Hats: birthday hats, paper crowns, historic hats, army and sports helmets

Inflatables: beach balls, punching bags, furniture, inner tubes

Keys: antique door keys, old locks, old door handles, handcrafted keys, key catalogs

Kitchen tools: scrubbing tools, antique ice cream scoops, unusual plastic utensils, sponges, antique toasters

Light bulbs: antique bulbs; decorator, commercial, old photographic bulbs

Mirrors: truck mirrors, old makeup mirrors, unusual mirror tiles, supermarket mirrors

Natural objects: shells, rocks, feathers, colors of earth, brick samples

Masks: disguise kits, industrial protective wear, surgical masks, antique gas masks, Halloween masks

Memorabilia: autograph books, old postcards, family photo albums, old greeting cards

Plastic items: rainwear, flowers, slide sleeves, menu holders, name tags, vacuum-formed wrap, unusual shrinkwrapped products

Printed art: old food can labels, antique playing cards, old posters, old board games, antique puzzles and mazes

Paper: unusual doilies, patterned napkins, giftwrap, wallpapers, envelopes, receipt pads, key labels, sandpapers

Plumbing: plastic pipes, accordian drain pipes, brass pipes, brass fittings, unusual hoses, sprinklers, washers

Rulers: architectural rulers, fashion rulers, engineering templates, chemistry stencils, wood rulers

Scales: postal, egg, talking, pharmacy

Souvenirs: anonymous diaries, antique coloring books, used school notebooks with students' doodles, souvenir postcards, Japanese and Chinese fans, antique writing desks

Stampers: antique children's printing sets, wood type, date stampers, embossing machines

Stickers: stamps, office labels, mailing labels, corporate seals, stars

Tin containers: antique lunch boxes, illustrated watering cans, sand pails, coin banks

Toys: windups, new and old pull-toys, new construction sets, plastic toy figures, art toys like Etch-a-Sketch and Magna Doodle, balls and block sets from different countries, contemporary blocks, marbles

Some other categories that I especially recommend include children's books (old and new ones, comic books, beautifully illustrated books); sculptural books such as pop-ups; books of figures to cut out, assemble, or dress; toys (for example, science-fiction toys; art-related toys, such as stamper kits; painted tin toys; old game boards); antiques and collectibles (old tools, hats, pitchers, bottles, buttons); foods (packaged candy, rows of lollipops, interesting gum wrappers, clear wrapping for foods, edible greeting cards, fancy chocolate boxes); illustrated menus and place mats; illustrated catalogs (for toys, department stores, clothing, paint, hardware items, housewares, fabrics); and natural objects such as leaves, dried flowers, rocks, shells, and branches. Collections may also include artworks and reproductions.

Artworks, art books, and reproductions in themselves form another category of items that should be frequently displayed and developed into a classroom library in art class to provide examples of visual beauty and to get students in the habit of learning from other artists about matters that are of concern to them in their own work. When we discover elements we like in the artwork of others, we begin to compare their work with ours. Our own artistic concerns are amplified and tested, and sometimes problems we have been considering are resolved by looking at someone else's work.

For example, when I first "met" Zandra Rhodes, it was love at first sight. While browsing through a used-book store, I discovered her fashion designs, and her work influenced my paintings for an entire year. My class listened intently as I described this first meeting and the intensity of our year-long affair, which led to a fruitful imaginary collaboration. My students were interested to learn how a painter can be inspired by the same book for a long time. My use of the book has varied from occasional browsing to intense exploration, through projections, cut-up photocopies, tracings, and redrawings until the work and its essential attractions have become clearer to me. As I come to understand it better, I isolate the ideas in it that are relevant to my own work. I showed the students what my work looked like before my study of Zandra and how it changed as a result of the experience. The discovery of an art book can have a profound effect on each artist. Where and how a book was discovered, the significance it has for the artist and teacher, the inspiration it has given, the pleasures of ownership, and the value of collecting beautiful books should be conveyed through the art lesson. Each book should represent a special discovery and a creative choice on the part of the art teacher. Groupings of books function as examples of the teacher's observations and interests. The general attitude of how each book is shared, the excitement and respect accompanying its showing, demonstrates the book's meaning to the teacher.

During the introduction to a new medium my students receive a museum and environmental tour through the pages of the most beautiful books I am able to assemble for the occasion. Examples are selected to demonstrate the wide range of possibilities inherent in each subject and to inspire through the beauty of the artwork and the quality of reproduction. The selection of books should reflect the teacher's concerns, as well as the students' range of interests. Thus, the study of color may include books on neon lights, color photography, and varied forms of body painting. Sculpture may be looked at through a book of tents, sand castles, or Henry Moore's works. This "introductory book fair" becomes a primary source of student independence. Browsing is encouraged so that each student may discover unique aspects of an art problem. After the introduction, selected volumes serve as a class library for the duration of the lesson.

Although it is useful to have students compare their works with the completed works of other students, it is most important to have them test their ideas against the best, the highest artistic models that they are inspired by. Conversations about what artists they admire and how they think their works relate to those of artists they find creates an ideal, a hero, while establishing a direction that one can work toward, against, and finally away from as one discovers a new model. Students need to look at other artists very often in this roundabout way to discover what their own work is about. We can give them opportunities to discover these special persons or special works on their own by providing an abundance of books and magazines for them to look through, since each artist talks privately and uniquely to another. In many make-believe exercises, I also have students imagine that they are holding a Japanese calligrapher's brush, or are guided by the spirit of Van Gogh in making their marks; that Picasso is holding their hand with his invisible one as they perform an artwork.

Coming in contact with great artists is exciting to students; it makes them feel that the world is wide open to them in all its visual possibilities and that they are members of the world of art. This identity with the art world is important, for all artists are lifelong pupils of their predecessors. The aim is not for students to copy the great artists but rather to learn how to incorporate the visual concerns of the artists they admire into their own works. Students have to understand what has already been accomplished in the world of art and to go actively on from there. The purpose of displaying artwork is not to teach students art history per se but to get them into the habit of continually referring to and thinking about great artworks as a way of learning and as a resource for their own artwork. If they get into the habit of consulting other artworks as resources, they may continue to do so throughout their lives.

Teachers should feel free to depart from the lesson entirely, at any time, to show the class new personal discoveries they have made. Students are always greatly interested in the teacher's personal finds, and by showing them our discoveries immediately, while they are fresh and new to us, we share our excitement with them and serve as living examples of visually alert artists. One time, for example, when I was buying new frames for my eyeglasses, my wife and I disagreed over the choice of frames, and so I brought the problem to the attention of my students. I was pleased to discover the wide variety of innovative types available and borrowed a catalog to illustrate some of them to my class. I also brought along all my old frames, which I had faithfully kept; some antique frames from a collection of mine; and some other examples of frames culled from an old Sears catalog. In addition, using loose wire, I fashioned several new sets of frames whose shapes were different from what I had on hand. The students and I spent the period discussing possibilities, trying on the glasses, and sketching each other's faces with different frames to discover how the shape of the frames affects the face and vice versa. We talked about the design of glasses as an art form and then broadened our discussion to other face coverings such as veils, safety goggles, disguises, and masks.

Thus, common experiences yield uncommon inspiration. With the teacher as model, students begin to realize that art is an important part of life—that art and life are connected. Visually informed decisions have to be made time and time again in a variety of real-life situations, some so routine that we do not think of them as visual choices.

CLASSROOM DESIGN

Everything surrounding students—the space, surface, and objects of a classroom—affects their work. We can therefore manipulate these surroundings to inspire interesting work. Our reaction to a space is influenced by past experience. Because students are accustomed to certain setups in the art room, rearranging it can have a profound effect on them. Teachers should be aware of the class's expectations, sometimes working with them, sometimes against them, redesigning the classroom to express the play idea and the art idea of the lesson.

The art room should be seen as a flexible canvas whose surface can be freely altered to communicate the objective of each lesson. Classroom space can be restructured by using lights, partitions, or obstacles, thereby indicating the steps to be taken to begin or complete an art problem or suggesting the scale of the work. Space can be restructured by making

- rows to use as paths, roadways, runways, or mazes, using classroom furniture, plastic hoses, drainpipes, bricks, stones, or tiles;
- barricades (obstacles, dividers, partitions), using insulation blocks, blankets, screens, or construction-site cones;
- mounds (stacks and piles), using pillows, inflatable objects, stuffed garbage bags, chairs, or lunch boxes;
- covers (tops), using sheets, dropcloths, parachutes, or umbrellas;
- tunnels (openings, peepholes, containers) using tables, tires, tents, metal shelving, or plastic screening;
- points of attention (spotlights, marked spots), using tapes, flags, lights.

Familiar surfaces can be covered, wrapped, framed, or altered in line, color, or texture, perhaps indicating feelings as well as ideas. Furnishings and other objects can be reorganized, added to, or removed, to create a particular frame of mind. Just as interior designers communicate through pattern and relationships and artists arrange their work space to suit the needs of their work, so the art teacher can suggest art ideas by changing the classroom space and its contents.

The design can be as simple or as elaborate as circumstances permit and as the needs of the lesson require. In schools where there is no art room and where teachers must bring all their "props and sets" with them, here is room for innovation in the use of lightweight, inflatable, disposable items. Rooms can be filled with projections, lights, and sounds, with a minimum of equipment. When simple props are used, more attention can be paid to dramatic presentation. Each situation is unique and has advantages and disadvantages that must be taken into account. It is true that art can be made anywhere: I have taught art from the back of my van, from inside a rented trailer called an Art Mobile, from a pushcart called an Art Cart, as well as from the rooms of other teachers and in my own studio. Art *can* be taught anywhere, but we need to understand the qualities of "anywhere" and use each space and place to its best advantage. Since no two spaces or teaching situations are alike, we must be able to size up the situation quickly and identify the resources (room shape, furniture, light, and so forth) that we can use, without feeling handicapped by what we do *not* have. Lessons can be planned to help any space come alive.

Each art space needs to be looked at with new excitement. A teacher who travels from class to class of course has disadvantages, but such a teacher has the advantage of encountering daily many new spaces to react to. A classroom of which a teacher has exclusive use for a long time can quickly become stale if the space is not revisualized daily and revitalized for each lesson. Teachers who have limited art resources are in fact not limited if they see the world as their resource. An unpleasant classroom or the lack of a permanent art room can even encourage teachers to find innovative solutions.

Each lesson need not require an elaborate interior design. If the art room is kept as open and uncluttered as possible, any change, even a small one, is quickly registered by the students. For example, a wet sheet recently dyed green and hung diagonally across the room on a clothes-line, illuminated on each side by differently colored lights, communicates color ideas to the students as it affects the space around them.

Less can be more, and simply making small-scale, inexpensive, yet unusual alterations in what children see, do, or experience in class can result in a very effective lesson. The teacher's way of speaking, moving, or pointing to something in a humorous or unusual way can help transform the classroom experience without requiring an elaborate stage set. Just about anything already present in the classroom can be used for props or supplies. One of my most memorable lessons developed from collecting all of the children's gloves one cold day. Children's glove designs have an incredible range of colors, shapes, and designs, since they are intended both for function and for entertainment, and our collection made a marvelous illustration of the variations possible within a single environmental form.

The means of transporting materials and other supplies to school can in itself become part of the presentation or a traveling exhibit. I have a van that I take from school to school, and I often start the class by inviting the children to visit the van. I can show them the kinds of preparations that the artist makes and the kind of collection that every artist must have, whether it is in the car, the studio, or the shopping bag—the creative arrangements of objects around oneself that all artists make. A van is not necessary, though; unpacking the items in a shopping bag, a suitcase, a shopping cart, or a little red wagon can be just as revealing.

I really think that rather than being disadvantaged, traveling teachers have an advantage over teachers who work in permanent classrooms. When I see art teachers walking or bicycling to school empty-handed, I wonder if they have gotten used to the convenience of having everything ordered in advance and shipped to them. The traveling teacher is more aware that everything that is exciting and beautiful—the museum, the landscape, the designed environment— has to be transported to school. Learning to collect, store, and transport displays and objects routinely is excellent training for all art teachers; we all should be in the "import" business.

Great artworks are often created in response to limitations, when the artist recognizes the limitations and responds to them creatively. I will never forget visiting my friend the painter Robbie Ehrlich, whose wall-sized canvases I had seen only in New York City galleries. When I visited his studio, I could hardly believe that he was able to work in what amounted to an attic closet, assembling the sections of the larger works in this incredibly tight space. For him, the limitation had turned out to be a creative stimulus. I have also noticed how my own paintings have varied, depending on whether I was working in a low-ceilinged basement, a long hallway, or out of doors. Traveling art teachers, who have to adjust to such "limitations" as smaller spaces, faster cleanup, or less control over the room, have to respond creatively and must pay close attention to all of the small details of the performance—the way they walk through the door or the surprises they may bring in their pockets, for example. They are forced to make innovative and economical use of all of the available resources. The results, designed by necessity, can be glorious in the end.

Whether the means used are simple or elaborate, teachers should constantly redesign the room, creating a setting that inspires both curiosity and enjoyment. The students should be able to think of the classroom as a magical space where we can see through walls, where the floor may be seen as the bottom of the ocean, where the ceilings open our view to the heavens; a space where teachers constantly make visual discoveries and encourage students to do likewise by example and by providing a rich and ever-changing environment.

To begin redesigning the classroom, teachers need to take a close inventory of the room: its size; shape; amount of space; colors of walls, floor, ceiling, fixtures, and furniture; types of surfaces; architectural features such as doors, windows, and closets, as well as the view from the windows; and furnishings. Smaller objects should also be examined: fire extinguishers, hooks, hangers, and doorknobs can all be made use of for their colors, forms, or other features. We can also consider what could be added to the existing environment to enrich it.

The shape of the art room should be understood and carefully diagrammed. This shape can be altered by simple modifications— insertions of objects, lighting, and the alteration of furniture, such as groupings, wrappings, and drapings. Such modifications give the space a new look and a new feel. They suggest pathways, movements, and the flow of activities. They can provide privacy or promote interaction. They may even communicate the quality of space itself: negative and positive space, foreground and background, depth and perspective. By such modifications—rearranging books or shelves to create temporary divisions, using string or partitions as dividers—the teacher can indicate the organization or structure of a particular lesson. Where should students look? How can certain aspects of a lesson be highlighted? These questions can be answered by the rearrangement of space. Such rearrangements, because they change the surroundings, will change how students experience the lesson. Each day they will be confronted with a new pattern through which they must move at a particular speed; a large form set in a small room will obviously dictate a certain set of responses. Depending on the needs of the lesson, the rearrangement can be subtle or aggressive. Whatever the changes, they are important as a means of teaching students the concept of space. Redesigning space is like creating a preliminary artwork, a "dry painting" that allows an art idea to be expressed in live space. The teacher must previsualize the idea to see how it can best be experienced three-dimensionally.

Just as the classroom space can be altered to communicate the concept of the art lesson, so can all the areas that surround and define the surfaces around the artwork (even the surface under or over the work) be altered. Floors, ceilings, windows, doors, chalkboards, shelves, and closets are all special canvases with existing patterns, colors, and textures that can be altered by additions of inspiring objects, coverings, and lighting. Surfaces can serve as a background to the art activity, or they can be treated as the center of that activity, with their own colors and patterns highlighted by special displays. Walls can be covered or painted, for instance, or floors temporarily covered with tiles, pieces of paper or carpet, or other materials, so that the lesson's idea—as indicated by changes in the room's surface—can be clearly understood.

Aside from redesigning the entire room, individual table areas, surfaces, and corners also can be redesigned. These areas can be draped with cloth and fabric; edges can be covered with unusual materials, shapes, forms, or powders. The furnishings in the classroom can be altered: They can be grouped, lined up, or stacked; treated as barriers or partitions; or used as easels or sculptural forms. All the details of the room must be kept flexible so that changes can easily be effected: Furniture can be turned upside down, wrapped, stacked, or perhaps removed altogether. Every piece of furniture in the room is a potential surface for work; students can work over, under, around, or next to tables, desks, chairs, even the trash can. They can take advantage of the light that a window lets in or the softly contoured wet space of a sink. The appearance and use of each piece of furniture is therefore open to redefinition.

Some teachers hesitate to rearrange the schoolroom to this degree, fearing disapproval. To them I would say that we imagine more limitations in school life than actually exist. Even beginning teachers will let you know in no uncertain terms which ideas will work in school and which will not, things that can and cannot be done with children. What we feel is possible may be closely tied to our desire to fit into a school system without being noticed, without risk. All these qualities, however, are not the qualities of the artist in relationship to society. Artists should not be afraid of the challenge of being different. It is not enough to tell our students that art deals with the extraordinary: This also has to be demonstrated by our treatment of the classroom, by its space and furnishings, and by our speech and actions. To risk moving tables and chairs allows the taking of chances in freely moving about shapes and forms in the artworks growing out of the classroom experience. While an unusual room situation will get the attention of administrators or other teachers who may respond with curiosity, it does not mean they will disapprove. It will certainly get the attention of the students whom the teacher seeks to inspire! Although it is more difficult and time-consuming to think of the art room as a stage set, as a flexible environment on which to inscribe art, the students who benefit from and enjoy it will also be understanding, and they will be eager to help to restore it by putting things back "in place."

The room design will be influenced by the other major elements in the lesson: the type of play activities that are planned, the material displays and other exhibits, and the type of "performance" that the teacher plans to give in presenting the lesson (see the section on performance at the end of this chapter). All of these must be coordinated through the lesson plan. Ultimately, room design becomes a matter of stage design, with the entire room visualized as a stage.

Examples of room designs are listed below:

- A drawing is made on a white wall using gray tape. Tape lines form a hopscotch board on the floor tiles next to the wall. A lesson on drawing on environmental surfaces is introduced.
- Walls are "papered" with papers and objects that are red. Shiny Mylar squares are placed on tables near the wall to reflect the colors. Bright red construction cones mark the path into the room. A lesson on color collecting is introduced.
- Tall black panels are leaned against the white wall. The chairs are covered in black plastic bags. A design for a lesson on geometric and soft sculpture is introduced.
- Pulleys are placed on the wall with lines connecting different surfaces of the room. See-through plastic sheets are hung from each line and a slide projector is used to project light through these movable screens. A lesson on discovering plastics as an art surface is introduced.
- The room's furniture is attached with chains that descend from hooks and hangers along the wall. A lesson on sculpture and movement is introduced.
- Squares of green outdoor carpet are placed on selected floor areas. Red ribbons hang from the ceiling. A wooden clothes drying rack stands in the middle of the room. A lesson on sculptural supports and displays is introduced.
- Hoola hoops are placed on plastic sheets on the floor. Sand, marshmallows, and water are placed inside. A lesson for exploring ideas for outdoor sculpture is introduced.
- Tables are lined up in front of the class door. Entrance is through the "tunnel" under the tables. The first view is that of an open umbrella, a tent, and a hanging parachute. A lesson of sculpting spaces and enclosures is introduced.

PLAY

Artistic knowledge is built from the analysis and evaluation of firsthand experiences and playful interactions with the environment. Artists play constantly, trying out new arrangements and designs not only with familiar materials like paint or clay but with any objects around them. They also play imaginatively, exploring fantasies, dreams, and images. Most adults are not supposed to play while they are working, but playing is, for artists, an essential *part* of working. The open and relaxed state of mind needed for making art requires a sense of freedom to experiment, to do whatever one wants to do with ideas, materials, and tools, without being restricted by rules and pre-conceived ideas—even one's own. When artists work, they seek the relaxed state of mind that permits all of their powers—physical, emotional, imaginative, and intellectual—free play. Artists play in preparation for a work, experimenting with ideas and materials that they have tentatively selected; they continue playing while making the work, freely rearranging as they get new ideas, and changing their minds

Form fantasies inspired by soap bubble plays in class.

entirely if necessary; and they play afterward, never regarding the "finished" work as the final object.

Because children's imaginations thrive on play, play can be used to help them create thoughtful and exciting works of their own. When students play, they can draw ideas from their own experience instead of narrowly following the teacher's lead. They become actively involved in class activities and are able to discover the meaning of each lesson by rethinking from a personal perspective the problems that the lesson presents.

The basis of each of my lessons is a broad *play* idea that at the same time involves a broad *art* idea. I choose an idea that I know my students will find intriguing from the beginning because it is a form of play that children always love to do. From the broad play idea at the heart of the lesson, I can also develop many other types of play during the lesson time—fantasies, movement play, play with toys, and so forth—that I also know from experience will please most children. So, for example, when I taught my elementary school students a lesson based on dressing-up play, exploring the art idea that through imagination and actions the artist can transform everything, I knew that the students would like the whole idea of getting dressed up and would be eager to try out the many costumes I had brought for them. To make it even more intriguing, I created a whole fantasy experience involving "identities" for us to enjoy. When the students entered the classroom, they found the room entirely dark, and they were escorted to their seats with flashlights. Suddenly, a spotlight came on, as I tried on a set of funny glasses, putting on different faces and identities, commenting on how each set made me feel. I opened a suitcase and began to display the dress-up clothes, explaining, in the meantime, that we had to go "underground" and develop new identities as a result of being pursued by an international ring of pirates. This gave me the most natural opportunity to discuss art as transformation, and later, after the students had dressed up, to talk with them about how it felt to become someone else and to encourage them to try drawing while they pretended to be this new character or person. At the end of class we had an art-party fashion show in which all of the students displayed their costumes and wore the artwork they had made, which provided a fine opportunity for discussing the whole lesson experience and for me to make a final statement about it. Although we did several different types of play during the lesson, all of them were related to the fundamental idea of transformation. We were working with some very sophisticated and important art ideas—and we were also having a lot of fun. This is the kind of lesson I try to create for all my classes: a lesson that combines a fundamental play idea and a fundamental art idea. (This is discussed in more detail in the section on lesson ideas in Chapter 4.)

Getting students to play is, paradoxically, one of the best ways of getting them seriously engaged in art. The genuine involvement that they feel when they play helps younger children, who tend to rush to finish, to slow down and investigate all the various possibilities for the artwork, as artists do. Older children can relearn the natural ability to make art. By playing out unclear or abstract art ideas with real forms, students gain a thorough understanding of the art problems they are exploring. When they play in art class, individual students recognize that they have valuable ideas and can make a contribution, and they find it worthwhile to develop the necessary skills.

Encouraging children to play throughout their art making does not in any sense imply that the teacher becomes a bystander. On the contrary, the teacher has a challenging and difficult job to do. Entering the child's imaginative world, providing an atmosphere in which children feel free to play, and designing lessons that challenge children to play as they learn about art requires research, innovation, and great creativity—the kind of creativity and imagination that art teachers have in abundance.

Preliminary Play

For students of all ages, preliminary play at the beginning of the period is especially important to establish an attitude of playfulness and experimentation that can be maintained throughout the class. Preliminary play is the initial research, the necessary investigation, the important shifting of materials and ideas, the experiencing of movements and images through which most of the important decisions about the artwork are made. Just as play allows the mature artist to discover beautiful colors, space, or lines before structuring them into an artwork, it allows children to see what is interesting about the lines of a hose or extension cord, the space of the classroom as one moves furniture and other forms around inside it, or the colors of found materials they are arranging. Play becomes a means of observing and rehearsing so that a better, more informed use of these elements can be made.

For students, preliminary play provides a pressure-free experience. Knowing their work will not be judged, they are more patient and take greater care in making their decisions. The time spent on preliminary play significantly increases the amount of time spent in creating the artwork, which, in turn, greatly increases the number of choices a student can make.

Play situations should be built into the lesson as a whole, with materials and situations set up to encourage play during and after art making, as well as before. Throughout the art making, teachers need to encourage children to approach materials and tools playfully. Many other forms of play also need to be encouraged in art class: playing with ordinary toys, verbal fantasizing, storytelling and poem making, dancing and other forms of movement, and performances such as putting on short plays or mime. Planned or spontaneous play experiences can occur at any point during the lesson, once teacher and students become experienced players, and the students' contributions are often just as imaginative as the teacher's or more so.

To encourage children to play, teachers should strive to make all of their own actions playful, demonstrating how artists play freely with everything in the environment. The students and the artist together are like magicians or jugglers who explore the possibilities of objects through manipulation, who consider forms in terms of unusual performance possibilities. They can become builders, constructing, stacking, putting together, or structuring forms from all kinds of things around them. They can become quick-change artists, wearing or trying on almost anything, coming up with unusual ways to examine objects by wearing them or disguising themselves with them. They can illustrate ideas of line by taking a ribbon from a girl's hair or unwinding a roll of tape or film. They can play with moving forms, such as doorknobs, window shades, or pulleys. They can assemble and take apart objects and they should feel free to make art in class in marking all types of surfaces with any kind of tools. Such playful manipulations can be planned as part of the lesson, but many are inspired on the spur of the moment by the things at hand.

The teacher also needs to feel free to play with fantasies, dreams, and imaginative visions. I especially like to use a variety of what I call "challenges," for preliminary play, in which children are asked to create by being challenged through various means such as:

> *speed*: working in 25 seconds, or faster than the speed of sound, or as slowly as a snail;
> *size*: the largest in the world, or small enough to be seen by a microscope;
> using (or not using) different body parts—only one's toe, opposite hands, blindfolded.

Challenges are unusual, and are deliberately designed to sound impossible, crazy, or even abstract, stretching kids beyond their usual ways of thinking and working, and engaging their imaginations in what they are doing.

Visually challenging instructions can be given whenever possible instead of technical directions. In instructing students, for example, to glue soft papers (napkins, lens tissues, etc.) on a drawing surface, we can ask them to "cover the stage with a soft, plush carpet," "a blanket of soft clouds," or "a fresh, thin layer of snow."

As the lesson progresses, the teacher "broadcasts" the students' findings, noticing and communicating unusual solution ideas, celebrating discoveries found publicly in students' art. In calling attention to unusual finds throughout the lesson, playful explorations receive support. In publicizing a new idea, the innovator has a chance to hear about it and learn from the teacher's reception while the entire class constantly receives new clues and ideas.

The teacher's ability to accept the fantastic, say the ridiculous, and think the unbelievable sets the stage for the student's playfulness. The teacher needs to be daring, independent of classroom routine, and open about what is possible to do in a school room. It may be possible, dignified, and appropriate for the art teacher to walk over twenty paper cups to make an idea come to life. Teachers can be playful even in approaching classroom routines like taking attendance, putting up signs, and distributing messages. Pointing out the window and wondering what lies beyond the clouds, or marching through the classroom as if a parade is following, enhances student discovery. It is the art teacher's actions that convince students that their dreams, fantasies, and imaginary play have a place in art.

Imagining and Pretending

The kinds of play that challenge children to use their imaginations and to dream fantastic visions are especially valuable for preliminary play, establishing an atmosphere in which play and children's ideas are welcome, and banishing the ordinary, everyday approach to experience. Verbal fantasizing and pretend plays, such as dramatic performances, can carry children beyond the ordinary confines of the classroom into a realm of new ideas and visions. As children talk about, write down, or act out their fantasies, they not only discover ideas and images for artworks but also become aware of their own creative and imaginative powers. The sense of power and ability gained through imaginative play, when children's dreams and visions are appreciated and praised, often carries over into their artwork.

In the classes that I studied, a very large proportion of the conversation consisted of instructions issued by the teacher to the students. Only a small proportion of the conversation was concerned with imaginative ideas. Yet the teacher's imaginative use of language can expand the scale, medium, complexity, or any other aspect of an artwork for the students. By calling for the most unusual, the most humorous, the most complex visions, teachers challenge children to move from the ordinary to the extraordinary. A challenge to make something that is the largest, wildest, most ornate, or most unusual thing of its type licenses the search for unusual visions: For example, children can imagine creating a thousand-legged monster as big as the art room in six seconds, or what it would be like if a concrete bridge changed into jello. When they think about printing, they can imagine taking impressions of the bottom of the ocean, the side of a redwood tree, or the pyramids. With the whole world as their resource, they formulate their prints first as visions, considering the widest and most exciting range of surfaces, processes, scales, and materials. Outrageous statements and unusual questions also challenge students to visualize. Playful, almost silly conversations set the mood for an uninhibited pursuit of unusual ideas and extraordinary images. Imaginative clothing designs may be inspired by talk of "chocolate-frosted clothing," and making up silly words for new shapes and colors can stimulate interesting form and color ideas. In placement exercises, for example, students envision the paper as a tennis court as they move shapes and colors from side to side. In play with surfaces, we imagine that the drawing paper is ice cold and we actually handle it with gloves and skate over it, inscribing our lines sharply in the ice. In another painting experience, we imagine the paper too hot to touch as this imaginary hot plate instantly melts our colors, which are the students' new "ice cream color" finds.

Through the creative use of language, ideas can be transported through different times and places, without boundaries. The students can approach art ideas as explorers or inventors, describing the unimagined and speaking of the unseen with remarkable clarity. They can pretend to be making their artworks in an underwater art studio, inside a video game, inside an artificial heart, or in paradise. They can pretend that they have fourth-dimensional vision, 360-degree seeing ability, or that they can draw faster than any other human being. They can pretend to be a cave artist, an African tribal sculptor, a world-famous cake decorator, or a toy designer. They can pretend to be a strange creature, such as a spider trained to paint, a crib mobile that comes alive, or the world's most feared dragon.

When students want to work at a faster pace, they place their motorized pencils in a higher gear or make believe their robot arms are speeding out of control. As the teacher promotes the feeling for surface and line, students are asked to choreograph their moves, making believe they are ballet dancers, or break-dancing on a stage. Each magic pencil is capable of making varied patterns by switching stitches as if it were a sewing machine, or making different impressions by working with an unusually heavy pencil or one that contains a secret charge of dynamite if not handled with care. When we use different body parts for making art, fingers may be emphasized by making believe they are small creatures crossing the surface. Or we use our full arms, making believe we have a plaster cast on as we are drawing. To encourage the use of the entire body, we use extension handles such as fishing rods, broom handles, vacuum cleaner tools with drawing or painting tools taped to them. In this way we can "sweep" or "vacuum" colors across the surface, aware of the possibilities for full body movement. With the imaginative use of language, technical limitations and time or supply limitations are removed, and inventive new beginnings to an artwork are developed. When preliminary ideas are playfully discussed, one also gets the helpful reaction of an audience, which can often shock a student into building away from one idea to others beyond it. Language helps to build bridges to experience: For example, the creation of a mental picture of a magic carpet can be assisted by an imaginary conversation concerning the carpet. The playful use of language also creates a sense of excitement and humor and, ultimately, commitment to the artwork.

Students can express their fantasies in various ways—describing them to each other orally, writing them down as stories or poems, acting them out as plays. Dressing up and role playing allow individual children to see themselves differently. Any kind of performance—an impromptu parade, a dance, mime, puppet show, a short skit or play—can help students discover their personal feelings and ideas. During performances, "observations" become first-hand experiences, and new emotions—such as feeling important, strong, ugly, or powerful—are explored. Behind a costume, mask, or puppet, children who are usually repressed come alive and move freely. Through the simplest props, ideas easily become fanciful, and thoughts that may not be displayed in everyday actions or even in drawings become accessible. The pretending activity also gives students a sense of power to change things: Those who are willing to try new things in a performance may risk more later when they turn to art. In preparing to be someone or something else, students make new impressions on a surface, searching for different tools and techniques that they hold and move with in new ways.

Play Activities

As described above, some of the best kinds of play occur spontaneously, growing out of the interaction within the class. Sticking rigidly to the lesson plan can prevent teacher and student from playing freely; rigid planning is foreign to the spirit of play. In planning the lesson, however, the teacher will have selected a fundamental art idea to explore in class and will certainly want to select beforehand some types of play that seem especially appropriate for the lesson. Since the list of the fundamentals or basics of art will differ from teacher to teacher, the basic plays for art teaching discussed in the following sections simply represent some of my own priorities. This selection is meant to stimulate the individual teacher's inventiveness in searching out new play areas—not to limit anyone to the types listed here. Anything in art that can be learned through playful activity can provide a category of play to use in class. For example, instead of identifying play activities in terms of broad art ideas such as line or color, one can build art activities around particular toys—dolls, toys that move, video games—or familiar types of children's play—building with blocks, playing house, dressing up. One can think in terms of playing with particular materials: paint, sand, water, stones. The important thing is for teachers to see very clearly in their own minds how the play that they encourage in art class relates to art ideas. Play in art class, as I have already stressed, is genuine play and genuinely enjoyable—but it is also a form of serious work. (Some specific suggestions about ways of developing play ideas are developed in Chapter 4, "Planning the Lesson.")

Line.   Line is a basic quality in human expression, an essential part of the thinking and planning of all visual artists, from painters to architects to choreographers. The drawn line is the means of planning ideas that, when enlarged or reformulated, become paintings, sculpture, or buildings. A good drawing, for example, is first and foremost a pattern of beautiful lines that symbolize, abstract, or trace movements, ideas, and emotions. Learning about line is not a matter of studying abstract or realistic art but of recognizing a basic structure common to all art, from a small sketch to a detailed outline of an entire city plan.

All art deals, in one form or another, with line quality and arrangement.

Very young children, as we have seen, use lines freely in their drawings to express feelings and ideas, but in school their experience of line drawing is channeled into mechanical exercises of penmanship. Through playing with line making in art class, students can learn how to use lines again to express their feelings and ideas, to see beauty in pure line and relearn the pleasure of making marks on a surface. Playful experimentation with line is essential for drawing but also, of course, very valuable for painting, sculpting, and print making.

I especially like to free up children's drawings by issuing imaginative challenges to them:

"Pass your drawing tool to your neighbor," I tell them. "Make believe the pencil weighs a ton—you can hardly lift it. Try drawing with it. Now pass it back. It's so hot you can hardly touch it! Can you work with such a hot tool without burning your hand? Pass it back to your neighbor, slowly. This time a criminal has hidden nitroglycerin in one of our pencils. It is ready to explode if it's not handled carefully. Please draw with care! Now back to your neighbor. Look! The tool is covered with slime, something yucky. Draw with it, but don't get it all over you!" The pressure of working fast and the excitement of the imaginative play often lets them draw much more spontaneously and expressively than they normally would.

Play with line should include playful experimentation in observing and creating lines in forms that bring the subtleties of line possibilities as close to the child's attention and manipulation as possible. Preliminary play with linear materials in which children experience the qualities of line physically, by handling and manipulating objects, is especially valuable. Line experiences may include play with continuous lines, such as a bright red extension cord, to discover different patterns. Lines, in the form of strings or ropes, can be suspended or stretched from a single point on a ceiling or wall and connected at predetermined points in a room space. Lines can be tied together to create a variety of connections and changes in segment or rhythm, as when, for example, strings or wires are attached to each other or to railings, fences, and other interesting linear materials. Lines can be intertwined or woven around other lines or around objects. Linear materials can create frames, boundaries, or wrappers around forms and spaces. Students can use tapes or ropes to draw on architectural surfaces such as walls, floors, or stairs. They can explore drawing with rigid lines formed by pieces of lumber, rulers, pickup sticks, or with free-flowing lines of ribbons, film, fishing line, and so forth. Linear structures such as model railroad tracks, plumbing parts, or Tinker Toys can be built, assembled from strips, and taken apart many times in a linear version of children's block playing.

To bring linear play even closer to drawing, students can play with the drawing paper itself. Folding, tearing, or merely manipulating the surface can generate line ideas that can be redrawn, traced, or expanded in a drawing. Line play can be notated through drawings and by sketching a series of changes through which the experiment progresses. Drawings based on rubbings, tracings, photographs, shadows, or video images of the children's line experiments can be made. Experiments should include creating three-dimensional drawings from two-dimensional sketches, as well as developing drawings from three-dimensional experiences. Three-dimensional line play helps to give a feeling for lines as structuring substances, and the experiencing of lines as surfaces. It also helps the child recognize the relationship between the graphic line and the existence of line in the environment and may inspire him or her to use unusual drawing surfaces or tools, and to create a variety of experimental drawings.

Children can play with line-making tools. Beginning with the variety of rulers used by architects, engineers, and designers and moving on to the stencils used in the different art professions, we find many forms and tools with interesting edges against which one can move a drawing or marking tool. Every pair of scissors or ruler has a different line-making potential, depending on its size and weight or on the speed and movement with which the user works. Mechanical line-making tools such as staplers, hole punchers, and label makers, and more complex tools such as typewriters, compasses, sewing machines, braille writers, and computers can also be explored.

Children can play with line-making toys such as Etch-a-Sketch, Electra Doodle, Spiro-Tot, and Magna-Doodle; they can study the lines made on television screens by video games or electronic drawing toys by tracing them, and can also work with the images made by slides and overhead projections.

The human figure—the body and its clothing—can be used as a ruler or line stamper. From the fine lines of fingerprints to the sculptural outlines of shadow projections, body tracings, or body wrappings, the folds of skin and garments and the changing lines of parts of the body in motion—all can be traced or sketched to become sources for line ideas.

One of the most valuable forms of play for learning about line is movement play. Children can learn to see line making in the widest sense by perceiving the body as a tool that is continuously making lines in space. Art is made by movement, and the lines that individual artists make in creating their drawings and other works are affected by the individual's feelings, ideas, sensory perceptions, and body rhythms, all of which are expressed in the lines of the artwork. Learning how they themselves make lines when they move their bodies in space or work with tools on any surface helps children to gain confidence and control in their art and to plan the movements they will use in making a work. A detailed discussion of the value of movement play for art making follows.

Movement. Artworks are a result of both *inactive physical states*—observation, contemplation, and visualizing—and *active physical states*. The inactive states guide the active states of art making and the two sometimes occur simultaneously. Paintings, for example, are visualized in advance, but then one moves in applying the paint, which itself moves across the surface. A drawing is made by a sequence of movements that results in a tracery of lines. The artist also moves around a sculpture, or back and forth toward and away from a painting, to view it, while working. It takes movement to set up forms or to make impressions on a surface. Sculpture can be designed to move beyond its maker by being motorized or driven by the wind. Movement can be implied or felt in a work, therefore, *as a result of its design, or by visualizing the movements it took to make it.*

In my art making and in my teaching, I put great emphasis on being aware of and planning the movement that will make an artwork. For my own work, I frequently visualize and even dance out movement possibilities before I begin. To enhance the breadth and freedom of my movements when I am painting, I may attach my painting tools to long sticks, which allows me to enjoy a great freedom of movement in space, feeling its rhythm, and also lets me become an audience to my own work as I view it from a distance. In my classes, the students and I frequently rehearse the movements for an artwork, draw pictures in the air, feel the rhythm of movements we are going to make, and picture their results.

The more aware we are of the movement that it takes to make a work, the more effectively we can communicate through art. When artists make works of art, they express through each work rhythms and movement styles unique to themselves—to their individual heights, weights, and temperaments. If students become aware of the movements that are used in making art and of their own unique movement styles, they gain control over materials and tools and are better able to plan their works. They also learn that materials and tools suggest the kinds of movement with which they can be used. If movement play is stressed in art class, rather than practice in traditional techniques, students develop a sense of freedom to mark all sorts of surfaces and alter forms in any desired way.

The most important kind of movement experiences that I use in my classes are based on the movements that children normally use when they play—simple movements such as crawling, creeping, running, walking on tiptoe, hopping, bouncing, sliding, jumping, stooping, spinning, rocking, climbing, skipping, balancing, swaying, and shuffling. Since my lesson ideas always involve some form of children's play, I can easily work in movements like these as part of my own "performance," and the children love to join in and do them too. With the aid of the unifying lesson idea (often a fantasy idea), we can move easily from the movement activities into drawing or painting the movements, with the movements leading naturally into art making. Students, for example, can stand on alternate feet, spin like a top, and then draw their movements. In climbing experiences, the drawing paper can be set up on a stair or on boxes to make the experience even more relevant in the artwork. Movement activities can also be conducted simultaneously with art movements so that we are drawing, printing, and painting at the same time as we are rehearsing movements. For example, what does a drawing look like when performed while touching one's toes, rocking back and forth, walking a tightrope, or stretching to reach the paper high on the wall?

Movement play may focus on specific body parts. Finger movements such as pointing, tracing, squeezing, rubbing, folding, cutting, scratching, snapping, tickling, and patting can be performed on art surfaces with appropriate tools. Hand and arm movement, including clapping, reaching, stretching, pulling, pounding, punching, sweeping, swinging, and swimming can be rehearsed and their images kept in mind as they are explored with art tools. Foot and leg movements, such as standing on tiptoe, standing on one foot, kicking, toe tapping, heel tapping, clicking the heels, and bending the knees, can be recorded with various art media.

Movement explorations can be developed around sensory qualities or ways of moving sadly, joyfully, quickly, noisily, silently, or hurriedly. Finally, we rehearse the directions of movements in the air and on the page moving up and down, back and forth, across and sideways, backward and forward, over and under, above and below, side to side, corner to corner, or in circles or spirals. These explorations help to develop awareness of our choices and actions in movement across a paper.

We also use make-believe movements as a source for artwork. As we draw or paint, I may say to the students, "Imagine that you are . . .

- an elephant (kangaroo, tiger, snail, etc.) stamping through the jungle (hopping across the plain, etc.) with light and heavy movements;
- someone ice skating (swimming, skiing, playing tennis) on an ice rink (in a pool, etc.);
- a dancer, waltzing (doing ballet, break dancing, square dancing), recording your dance visually;
- a machine—a computer (vending machine, typewriter, sewing machine), recording the different patterns of your movements (sewing stitches, etc.);
- a farmer plowing a field (a steam-roller driver smoothing the earth for a new road, a gardener cutting grass with a mower, a mailman driving a dog sled), that is, different patterns and directions of movement, including spontaneous and random moves, as opposed to patterned and controlled moves;
- playing a violin (piano, drum, etc.), noticing the sound one makes as one moves across a surface, and the possibility of varying these sounds with different movements and pressures."

Movement play may stress the moves made by the art tool itself when it is imagined to be some other object or creature and used to interpret make-believe movements. For example, the tool becomes a jumping bean, an ice skate, or a mouse.

A principal tool in movement experiments is a flexible body that responds to sensory experience, to materials, surfaces, spatial organization, and to the environment in general. When children dance out imaginary movements before or during working, they are able to draw on their stored knowledge of the look and feel of movements and their enthusiasm for them. When they pretend to be a robot set into motion by a giant wind-up key, a showhorse jumping over the drawing paper, a worm digging into the paper, a bumblebee flying over the paper, a goldfish swimming under the paper, or (for double moves) a kangaroo playing soccer, a hoola-hoop-dancing gorilla, a Ping-Pong-playing cat, or a juggling snake, the patterns and rhythms of free movement in space may be carried over to the handling of art materials, and the lively mood that such play inspires extends into the art-making process.

When the children dance or act out the movements of an animal, a machine, or an imaginary creature, they are feeling from within the shapes that their bodies are making and the emotions involved—

power as an elephant stamps, joy as a horse leaps—and they are observing, and responding to, the movements of others as they dance or act out a role. All of these feelings and observations help them to work freely later when they are painting or sculpting the human figure or animals or other forms. For dancing, of course, we like to add music, drums, or other sounds—another sensory dimension that helps everyone to feel the rhythms and get fully involved.

Examples of movement exercises are given in the sample lessons in Chapter 4.

Dance is especially valuable as preliminary play for drawing. When children become aware that the body itself is continuously making lines in space, they can take this experience back to their drawing, becoming far more aware of the pattern of movement required for a good drawing. By helping them to view drawing as a dance—a line-making performance—we can focus their attention on the act of drawing and on line making as the principle content of any drawing. We can also help them to avoid the overcontrolled, limited drawing movement that they have learned in penmanship lessons and the tendency to use and hold drawing or painting tools as though they were pens. Children need to relearn the use of drawing and painting tools freely and expressively—to make the lines of their drawing or paintings "dance" over the surface. Performing or dancing the movements of line with the whole body (sometimes with tools in hand) helps the performer get in touch with the sensory aspects of the act of painting or drawing before the lines become artistic images and to become aware of the feelings expressed in the dance. Each line needs to be felt, experienced in its making, before it can communicate itself as an impression of life.

In line-performance exercises, space should be considered something to be moved upon (or through). The stage or surface used can be a free and open field—a meadow of grass or an open field of soft paper spread over the floor—or it may have well-defined edges marked out on the floor in geometric patterns that shape the movements of this "stage." The texture of the stage can be varied, to make children more aware of the texture of the surfaces on which lines and impressions can be made. It may be a thick, resilient, bouncy material such as foam rubber or carpeting, or a hard one; it may be rough or smooth, shiny or dull (formica, plastic, vinyl).

Line ideas can be danced without tools in hand:

- drawings made in space with one's body through pointing, with fingers, pointers, flashlights, and so forth;

- drawings made by stepping in mud or water, or walking across snow;
- drawings made in the air with a jump rope or a Slinky toy.

By avoiding paintbrushes and letting children experiment with applying paint to surfaces in other ways, we can make them aware of the many different ways of making paint move and of how their own movements affect the color patterns they make. They can try letting paint drip, splatter, flow, run, spread, and soak into a surface. They can try out the effect of dripping it from different-sized containers, with different kinds of apertures, from different heights and at various angles, with paints of varying consistencies. They can pour it from spoons or through funnels or tubes; they can dip napkins, fabric, and other materials into paint. They can work the paint directly with their hands or fingers, moving it with breath or with gloves (plastic, cotton, surgical, work, or baseball gloves). They can apply it with brushes not intended for paint—hairbrushes, toothbrushes, vacuum cleaner brushes, scrub brushes, shoe brushes; they can put it on with sponges or spray it on; they can spread thick paint with knives, bricklayers' tools, venetian blind slats, or spatulas. A wide variety of types of paint should be available, from house paints and stains to nail polishes and Jell-O, and a variety of surfaces on which to paint. These can include paper goods—napkins, cereal boxes, place mats, adding-machine rolls, wallpaper; household objects—lightbulbs, floor tiles, jars with labels, vacuum cleaners; fabrics—old ties, tablecloths, shower curtains, lamp shades; and building materials—insulating boards, ceiling tiles, bricks, and shingles. These should include surfaces that absorb paint, others that keep it on the surface or even repel it, and rough, smooth, or shiny surfaces. By working paints with so many different movements and using such a variety of tools and processes, children get away from trying to "write" colored images with penlike movements of a brush on paper. They learn to pay attention to the physical qualities of the paint and surfaces themselves and to adapt their movements to the materials and processes they are using.

Learning about the feeling of different surfaces by dancing over them is valuable for print making, too, and children should also be encouraged to explore the textures of all sorts of surfaces with their hands. They should feel the textures of printing inks and other printing pigments and work with them before using them for printing. They can learn to view the human body as the principal print-making tool—a surface for printing with—by making fingerprints (pressing their fingers on a stamp pad and making rhythmic movements with their fingers, as if moving across the keyboard of a piano), hand prints, lip prints, or footprints (using graphite powder and exploring dance movements by stepping across sheets of paper). They can become aware of the body as the source of pressure and movement as one brings two surfaces together and fuses them in the printing process. As materials are being pushed together, students can explore a variety of movements: using different pressures, pulling, pushing, rubbing, scraping, and stamping—in order to define soft or hard edges, and make light or dark impressions.

Dance, mime, and other performances help children to sculpt the human figure by letting them feel the shapes and lines that their own bodies make as they move and by letting them see the bodies of others in motion. Children can pretend to be dancers, soldiers, or athletes as movements are interpreted and discussed as sculpture. The addition of costumes and props can call attention to specific features of the figure—masks and makeup to the face and head, for example, or gloves to the hand, or costumes to the lines of the figure. Instead of dancing, they can pretend to be statues, freezing in place. They can manipulate puppets or dolls. They can set up Star Wars figures and imagine them in performance. Or, they can pretend to be these figures as they march or drive their vehicles through the classroom. Through this play, students begin to see sculpture as the choreography of human forms in space and experience becoming human sculptors and directing other play and other human sculptors. To record the images made in the movement exercises, they can sketch them, mold the body with foil or other molding materials, trace shadows, or videotape performances.

Color. Children are usually given prepared sets of colors to work with, so they do not know that artists invent and make colors. They also are not aware of the variety of colors that can be observed in the environment or mixed for working in art. Students need to learn that color tones and values are continually open to change, to see things in color, to create color ideas in their imaginations, to make beautiful colors themselves, and to find constant joy in new color discoveries.

Students can search for colors in the environment by examining the placement of different colors in a room or on a street. A brick wall viewed from the classroom window may afford students a long-term experience of noting its color changes at different times of day, in different weathers, and in different seasons. Students can be asked to collect samples of colors to bring to class, and their finds can be used for discussion and for color play in class. For example, they can sort dots of found color into clear plastic bags and arrange them in stacks or rows, hang them in space, or place them against backgrounds of other colors. Students can arrange flowers, prepare a salad of different colors, or set a table with brightly colored Fiesta dishware. The strategy of providing colored objects for students to arrange is especially valuable—painted clothes pins, for example, can be lined up, stacked, or tied together in various patterns. Students can add long pieces of painted tape to walls, floors, or various objects, arrange colored stickers, plastic paper clips, fabric swatches on graph paper or on pieces of wallpaper that have continuous patterns.

The color of any surface to be covered—even a white canvas or a piece of white paper—needs to be recognized as color before one applies another color to it. Working with a given or found color allows students to concentrate on the process of changing the colors of various surfaces. Students can explore how colors look against or upon various surfaces by adding the colors to them. Using color swatches that can be taped to things, or stickers, or resurfacing something by adding a newly painted section of paper or fabric will help the child experience color changes. A chair may be repainted, or a second tablecloth placed over the first; swatches of color may be added to a field of grass; or a section of wallpaper may be painted over. Through adding color to an existing color or color scheme, children can experience new color contrasts or balances. By repainting surfaces, they can begin to be aware of how colors, surfaces, and forms are related. They can also explore how a color changes under various kinds of light, using colored light bulbs, color gels, painted transparencies, and light filters.

Through experiments in mixing their own colors, students can learn that colors are made, that color tones and values are continually open to change, and that these are important choices in the planning of an artwork. In mixing colored paints, they not only learn formulas but acquire an ability to regulate and alter a color, leading it through a variety of changes. Specific mixing games can be developed to initiate investigations: Adding a particular color to all others; adding black and white to all mixtures; seeking the most unusual color, the deepest shade, or the brightest or the warmest color are useful in beginning mixing play. Using mixers, blenders, test tubes, funnels, and sample bags of color allows the notion of searching for color or inventing new colors before the artwork is begun. Collecting color fragments from objects and photographs and then trying to reproduce these through one's own mixtures helps students to develop color ideas and the idea that color needs to be researched. When used as preliminary play before painting, such exercises help to make the preparation or planning for colors a conscious, planned process related to the act of painting. Creative ideas continue to ferment in the very important initial contacts during the selection of colors and the actual mixing process, both of which may expand the original, or intuitive, thinking about the painting.

Form.   The flight attendant handed out the usual airline snack: peanuts wrapped in foil, and a soft drink. Little did she realize that out of this modest meal great forms would be created. After she had finished her snack, the little girl next to me carefully folded her orange napkin and carpeted the fold-down table with it; then she put other pieces of napkin, shaped into twisted forms, inside the clear plastic cup, now turned upside down. Around the plastic dome and on top of the carpet she set up shiny, shaped-foil forms, displayed with the care of a Japanese gardener. As the child lovingly admired her creation, an unappreciative flight attendant who was passing, seeing this "trash," snatched the magic garden setup before we could stop her and took it off to throw away. Children's informal play with form is a significant means of generating art ideas. Some suggestions for form play to use in art teaching are the subject of this section.

Whatever art medium they work with, artists today exhibit their awareness that form exists everywhere. They also express their personal preferences for certain types and qualities of form by exploring them in their work, and conceptualize form ideas, alter forms, extend them, and see new possibilities in them.

Student experiences in studying forms should lead to seeing beauty in all kinds of forms, developing personal areas of interest in unique forms, learning to play creatively with forms and to change and alter them, and learning to develop form ideas. Initial learning experiences can be activities that focus on observing, describing, and categorizing forms. At the introductory stage, we try to show students the vast extent of the form possibilities that exist all around them in the everyday world and how to recognize, within that vast field, form categories that reflect similarities and differences. Collecting forms of all kinds is an excellent way to begin this learning. Teachers' descriptions and exhibitions of their own collections provide an incentive and challenge to students to join in the adventure of discovering forms, which can be brought to school, compared, and categorized during show-and-tell sessions.

Students should be helped to see beauty and interest in all types of familiar objects, from soda bottles, paper clips, expressways, or objects selected from the grocery-store shelf to the carvings of a plough or a sandcastle on the beach. In categorizing forms, students can decide, for example, whether forms are hand- or machine-made, old or new, functional or decorative, geometric or natural, soft or hard, and can develop collections in the areas of interest to them. A student's collection of old appliance knobs from television sets, radios, fans, and stoves was an unusually elegant collection of plastic sculptural forms.

Form observations can also be gathered by studying how forms are related to their environment—for example, how forms relate to the ground, how they lie or stand on the floor, how they can be erected on a base or on legs, how they can be propped up or stacked in a space. One can also examine how forms can be attached to the environment—hung or suspended from walls or ceilings, for instance, by pulleys, hangers, levers, or strings. One can explore how forms can actively move, by floating, rolling, or spinning in space.

Another way to study form ideas is through observing displays. A store, for example, or a museum, can be considered a vast display of forms, which may be neatly stored or sequenced into compartments, as are candies in a chocolate box. A form can be framed by a plate or a tray on which it rests—a dinner plate, a lunch tray, or a jeweler's case. Forms may also be arranged in larger open areas, as football players are, for example, when they make their formations and use their prescribed plays.

Forms can be studied by observing containers and packages. They are often "packaged" or surrounded by space or by another layer of skin or materials. Forms can be displayed by their packaging—soap pads may be packaged in a plastic bag, its ends pulled loosely or tightly around them to make a new form of the container. Forms can serve as containers for other forms: A hamburger is covered by its sculptural fast-food carton, which may be in turn stacked into structural forms that are themselves, in turn, inside a building form. Often the cover of a container describes, through pictures and forms, what is inside it. Sometimes one container can be used to house several units of a form, or it can serve to separate and organize forms within it. Such containers include lunchboxes, fishing tackle containers, or a restaurant salad bar. Pockets in clothing, folders, envelopes, bags—all include interesting subcategories of materials and forms. For example, shopping bags, vacuum cleaner bags, bread and clothing bags, although they are all bags, are different types of containers, taking their shapes from their contents, as they are filled, stuffed, or inflated. A package itself, then, can make an excellent form study if we examine the supporting or structural materials and the stuffing or contents.

Covers for manufactured forms such as toasters, mixers, or typewriters, or for the human body—our clothing—can also be studied.

Besides observing and collecting forms, children learn about forms by actively playing with them. Artists can play with individual forms or can experiment with positioning or grouping them within a setting such as a surface, space, container, or area of light, or by assembling or disassembling them. Children's play involves the forms with which they are most familiar, including the human form—their own bodies—as well as dolls, puppets, and toy soldiers. The other main area familiar to children is the general category of toys. Forms are best studied when they are played with actively—when the individual is free to move them, balance, package, cover, wrap, eat, display, juggle them, as well as feeling free to move around the form to observe it from three dimensions, and alter it as desired. Such active play includes water, sand, and block play, which can be extended into play with all forms. These familiar early childhood play activities can be studied as the basics for many adult forms of play and art. Sand dwellings in Asia can be studied as well as sand play by other artists. Block constructions form igloos as well as skyscrapers, and can be explored through play with construction materials such as wood, bricks, and stones. Water play can examine the shapes of man-made reservoirs from swimming pools to lakes and canals. To encourage active play with forms, the teacher can suggest using everyday as well as unusual movements related to manipulating form, in materials and spaces. Packing a sandwich for lunch or eating an apple, an ice cream cone, or a large potato chip can follow the sequence of forms being made through a routine action. Deflating an inner tube or hammering a gutter may involve more unusual materials and play to discover forms.

Children love making "setups," and can playfully organize forms by arranging them in boxes or by displaying them on stairs, on a make-believe store counter, or inside an empty glass fish tank. Different environments, from outdoor to indoor settings, transparent or closed, will vary the way forms are played with. Playing with forms in water, inside a drawer, or on a hill suggests different play, forms, and organizations defined by the place and surroundings.

Other opportunities for playing with forms include becoming a form oneself or imitating forms with our bodies. Forms may be studied by observing steps, sequences, and changes in a form as a result of actions such as moving it, taking it apart, breaking it, or filling it with air or water.

The study of forms can begin with exploring individual forms by stuffing, inflating, wrapping, folding, or carving pieces in the same or in a variety of materials. This can be followed by a study of how several forms may be connected, assembled, systematized, or displayed, and related to settings or to environments.

Forms can be examined as they exist inside and outside spaces or containers, from working in a box to arranging forms in the interior of a whole room. Exercises can include varying floors or bases or using different modes of hanging, clipping, and attaching or floating forms in space, or different ways of having forms stand or move in a space, to see how the way in which the form is attached, erected, or hung relates it to the setting. Through sketches, tracings, wrappings, or examination of the shadows of forms, differences in shapes, silhouettes, and surface positioning can be examined. Different categories of forms such as covers, containers, hanging attachments, or assembled displays can be discovered.

One of the most important things to remember is that a great deal of display with found objects is a relearning of the original joy that children have in playing with pots and pans or arranging their teddy bears when they are very young. The joy of playing with forms simply needs to be rekindled, as new forms and new spaces and materials are introduced.

Children have many more observations, collections, and even everyday experiences from which to discover their form play. Here is a short checklist to use with students:

- Playing with a form's surface can include covering or layering forms with materials such as fabrics, plastics, tiles, or stones. It may include digging into, drilling, puncturing, or cracking a form's surface, which is hard or soft. Forms with interesting surfaces may be collected.
- Building from a variety of surfaces such as grass or from sculptural structures such as a ladder. Form play can take place with clay, rocks, bricks, or aluminum cans. Vertical surfaces such as walls can also be played on with pegboards, hooks, and vertical attachments.
- Building within a space may include manipulating forms within a given area or container, such as a crate, carton, file drawer, or stage. Lights, space dividers, and fabrics may be added to the arrangement of forms.
- Changing the meaning and context of forms may involve selecting an object that has a certain use and quality and recreating it as a new form, perhaps in a new setting. For example, a simple table may be altered and moved to become a cave, a camper, or a radio.

- Attachment play can be devised for clipping, sewing, tying, or stringing forms together, creating different joints and connections. Unusual hangers, rollers, clothes clips, hinges, springs, and pulleys can change the form's relationships and appearance.
- Dismantling play can allow a single object to be taken apart, broken, disassembled, cut, or eaten as new arrangements, assemblages, and forms are created.
- Playing with supporting structures involves using three-dimensional materials as supports, stands, or armatures. Wheelbarrows, carts, and shelves can be used as bases for form setups.

Form play generates visual ideas that students can further conceptualize and translate into other art forms. In playing with Ping-Pong balls or potato chips, play with forms can be documented in artworks or be the inspiration for new forms in different scales, materials, or subjects. As Claes Oldenberg's life-sized potato chips in plastic and Wayne Thiebaud's painted cakes in a bakery-store window indicate, contemporary artists' original inspirations exist in a variety of three-dimensional forms and form arrangements before they become artworks.

PERFORMANCE

Just as contemporary artists think of artworks as the result of particular movements made by the artist, so they have especially emphasized that artworks are the result of a creative performance by the artist—a performance that is preserved in the finished work. An artwork expresses a specific creative event in the life of the artist. In responding to the work, we respond to it as to a performance, seeing not only the end product but the way the work was made. The work calls our attention to—rather than concealing—the materials, movements, and creative acts that were needed to make it. Many artists today are strongly aware of the relationship between the visual arts and the performing arts—drama, dance, mime, and music.

As visual artists, we art teachers are aware that all human gesture and movement is expressive. The way teachers stand and move before their classes, therefore, is also expressive, and so is the way we dress and speak. For academic subjects in which the content is primarily verbal, it may not be too important for a teacher to make use of the visual effect of gesture and movement, or the dramatic effect of costume, language, and entrances and exits—although such ways of communicating can certainly help to enliven any class. In art class,

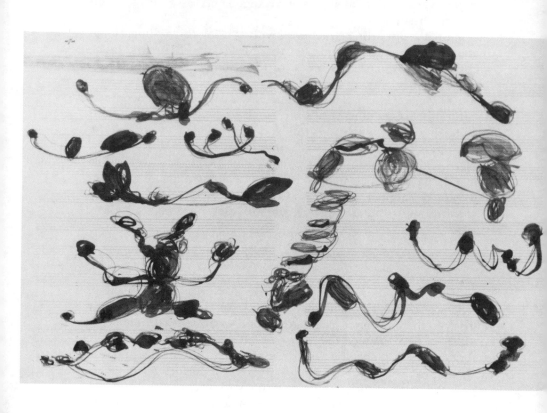

*Imaginary music score based on
a study of children's dance.*

where we want students to be aware of *all* of the visual aspects of their environment, we need to be aware of the teacher's actions and movements before the class as a form of visual communication—for it certainly is one. However we choose to move and speak before the class, we are making gestures, using body language, and giving a performance of one kind or another.

As artists, we understand the power of art of all kinds to speak indirectly to people, expressing ideas and emotions more powerfully than any direct "telling" or teaching can. By planning the art lesson as a performance by the teacher, in which all of the elements emphasized in the lesson—displays, room design, material design, and play ideas— as well as the teacher's personal movements, dress, and language are part of a creative whole, a unified artistic statement, we speak to the class with all of the artistic means that are available in the classroom environment. When a lesson becomes a performance, the lesson as a whole may be thought of as a work of art, and the teacher has clarified the relationship between art teaching and art making: The roles of the teacher and the artist are united.

In planning a performance, we begin with the play idea and the art concepts that the lesson is intended to convey. The play and art ideas suggest the sort of props we might want to use. For example, in my food-design lesson, the food theme suggested my performance as a "cook" mixing colors, and the presentation of the art materials and tools as food displays and restaurant items. The lesson idea also helps us to imagine the room design—in this case, designing the room as a collection of food stores and restaurants. For the performance, the entire classroom may be thought of as the stage or setting for the performance. The types of play we want to emphasize for the lesson will suggest particular dances or fantasy ideas to be talked about or acted out. For a lesson on the color red, for example, we might want to use a poem on the subject, as well as wearing red clothes and painting with red paint.

The teacher's acting out of an imaginary role is often an excellent way of demonstrating experimental play with materials or of starting off some other form of play that is intended to draw the children into the action and make them want to experiment too. For example, in a lesson about light and shadow, the room is darkened and objects in the room are set up to be awakened by the light. White eggs are placed on styrofoam sheets. Styrofoam balls are placed in white cardboard boxes and white images of human heads are placed in front of white cardboard sheets. With the accompaniment of music and magic incantations, student dancers greet the light by moving around the set-up forms with flashlights as they discover each form and its shadows. A great many of the teacher's performances are of this type: The teacher, by acting out an art idea or using materials and tools in a playful and physically active way, attempts to draw the students into the play activity through his or her own example. Whatever art idea the lesson explores, the teacher's performance must be a form of contagious play, fun and exciting, so that children not only enjoy watching but want to join in themselves. The tasks should be simple enough so that everyone can join in without elaborate explanations. Taking a magic-carpet ride or a make-believe train ride around the room simply requires imagination. Using familiar toys and games ensures participation. Using familiar objects in new ways helps to create a sense of surprise and eagerness: For example, children are eager to try painting by dipping a ball into paint and then bouncing it, or by dipping the sinkers of a fishing rod into paint and then onto a painting surface. Working on the floor with marbles or tops or trying out hoola hoops or blowing bubbles in large, open communal spaces attracts many children. All are interested in food play with attractive edibles such as marshmallows, jelly beans, and spray frosting. Dressing up and fantasy play invites children to dress up too and take on roles, and lets other fantasies emerge. Communicating with sound effects, imitations, or pantomime also evokes children's play instincts. The teacher's willingness to demonstrate vulnerability as a player—performing, for example, as a rather incompetent magician or juggler—invites others to try their skills. Using humor, exaggeration, outrageous challenges, and far-out language, the teacher becomes a willing player and a make-believe guide to anywhere.

Sometimes the teacher's performance is not intended to draw students into the action immediately but to make an instructional function more interesting. In other words, it is a playful performance of the role of *teacher*. For example, the business of displaying objects to the class can suggest amusing roles for teachers to play—they can pretend to be game-show hosts holding up prizes, or fashion models who explain how clothing and makeup were selected, or any other role that the situation naturally suggests. Teachers can become jugglers in balancing forms or fabrics. Magicians can change colors or pull things from hats or pockets. Ventriloquists can interview paintings or make brushes talk. Clowns may look at objects upside down or inside out.

On occasion, I pose as an archeologist, explaining to the class that this is my hobby. I "discover" a dinosaur bone (a chicken bone, which I sometimes have buried underground or hidden somewhere in the room), demonstrate my find, and describe my adventures in finding it.

I tell about how I utilize the form in my art. The experience leads to an explanation of how artists have to search far and wide for ideas and how artists search for materials. Sometimes I put on an old leather coat with big pockets to create a make-believe celebration of the anniversary of the time I left Hungary. I speak to the students of this special coat, which kept me warm while I fled over the border, and pull out from its pocket many momentos, to show how this pocket became a suitcase for all my important possessions. Next I show them examples of my own artwork relating to this subject. This performance ends in a discussion of how the subject and themes of art must have personal significance to the artist. Sometimes I put on my chef's hat and apron and mix colors in old pots on a make-believe stove. As I play my role, I stir in colors, discovering new "foods"—soups or sauces buried underground or hidden somewhere in the room. In our conversations, I try to describe to the students the experimental attitude needed for finding new colors, telling them that new colors can still be made and that colors in painting need to be discovered and, in fact, inspired. Such roles grow out of the teacher's literal role in displaying objects and in demonstrating or discussing art processes, but, through the use of imagination and humor, avoid the serious instructional stance that so easily turns off imaginativeness and playfulness in the children.

Even simple props and costumes help us to get into our roles. Wearing a crown or holding a teddy bear, we really feel like performers. By covering our heads with diapers, lamp shades, or surgical gloves, we can communicate the different possibilities for head coverings and act out the discovery of different types of objects and materials to be used in making masks.

The teacher's movement is a basic tool for communicating with students. As artists, we react to materials through our movements: We display our interest in objects and forms by our handling of them. We also react to students' discoveries and ideas through our movements, which can express interest, support, and approval. Indeed, the strongest gesture of support may be one not of words but of movement, for it is through such movement that our evaluation of students' works is confirmed or contradicted. We also express our enthusiasm for the lesson in our movements. To be sure that our movements are conveying what we intend, teachers need to evaluate their own performances through videotapes, photographs, and mirror exercises and, if improvement is needed, take lessons in acting, dance, or mime. Other sorts of movement training, such as fencing, can also be helpful. Speaking through visual things is natural for the art teacher. Thinking through images and props instead of lecturing is often comfortable even for a shy teacher. Talking about his or her own work, even the shyest artist comes to life.

A performance does not have to be an elaborate production to be effective. A single fantasy idea, or a single movement idea, for example, can suggest all sorts of related stories, dances, toys, or processes that could be used for the class, but we do not want to offer so many activities and "acts" to watch that students are distracted from the main idea. The skill in performance is to choose the types of performance that will best express the art idea of the lesson, in the most economical way. We must make sure that the performance as a whole is clear and coordinated—that the teacher's "role" *fits* with the "props" (materials and displays) available or that the room design permits the kind of dance movements or dramatic actions that are planned. A room design that is visually effective but does not permit freedom of movement without things getting knocked over, for example, is inappropriate for a lesson that demands free movement, just as it would be as a stage design for a play with a lot of physical action. The relative importance of the various elements of the performance will vary with the lesson idea, too—masks, for example, might be a relatively minor element in one production but a major one in a lesson concerned with drawing the face. The important thing is for the teacher to feel free to use any of the elements that can contribute to a performance as they are needed (including coming up with them on the spur of the moment), not feeling inhibited by the teaching role, and to learn to select those that are most effective for the immediate situation—not just the ones that are the most dramatic or fun to do. The ones that are used must be clearly relevant to the lesson idea.

For example, here is a description of performances that I used for the lesson "Audiences for Contemporary Art Experiments in Sounds, Movements, and the Visual Arts." The lesson began with chairs placed toward the center of the room, where several tables were pulled together. On each table was a selection of simple instruments such as cymbals, rattles, a flute, bells, and a synthesizer. In the same display were also hammers, a hairblower, noisemakers, and a toaster. I entered with a conductor's baton in my hand. The lesson began with two pieces of preliminary play. One was an original score consisting simply of sound effects made by playing with the displayed instruments, which students interpreted on music sheets. The second play of movement developed from watching the conductor move rhythmically as well as in different shapes and directions, which was interpreted through pencils tied to pickup sticks (batons). Each sound effect and movement exercise tended to produce a dialogue of sound effects and moves from inspired students who started to join in using the instruments and moving.

To begin the next part of the lesson, I began to relate a story of a recent visit to the School of Music at Indiana University. I observed a senior recital of contemporary music that began with a packed hall. The violinists and pianist not only played on their strings and keyboard, but explored all parts of the instruments not traditionally used for playing. As the exposition of unusual sound progressed, the audience began a mass exodus to the doors. Although knowledgeable in the field of music, the listeners were not ready to take an excursion into the new, or find out what else music could be. I told the students that we must hear this music to appreciate it, but that unfortunately I did not have a tape recorder with me, so I would conduct them through the piece. I proceeded to give instructions to the students to prepare their instruments and follow the conductor: "And now we will play the score entitled 'Music to Walk Out On.'" As an aside, I described my own experiences, as an artist, of audiences who came to my show— busloads of tourists who moved quickly into the exhibit and walked out just as quickly. What is new in art (or in art education) is frequently not understood and even rebelled against by audiences. A discussion period followed, in which questions were raised about what artworks would look like that audiences would walk out on. This became the individual task during the lesson. Students searched for the most unusual tools, shopped for the most outrageous materials, and tried the most unthinkable techniques as they began work.

Another performance was part of a lesson called "Pattern Printing (Fabric Design Experiments)." In preparation for this experience, the students were going to do a special artwork that would require them to wear the most unusual clothing they could find at home. The classroom setup included a table with a sign "The Fabric Store," where samples of materials such as rolls of white paper, newspaper, plastic sheets, and wallpaper rolls were available; another table called "The Tailor Shop," where tracing wheels and carbon paper were used as tools for pattern design; and a third table, called "The Fabric Printshop." My story to the class began as I unpacked a suitcase of my clothes, explaining that a most awful thing had happened at home. My daughter, looking at the clothes that I was wearing, told me that I was old-fashioned and "not with it in the eighties." I appealed to the class to help me in changing this image, explaining that although I have a great love of wild colors and patterns, I seem to select the most conservative things to wear. Could they change me into an eighties personality? Then I gave them a slide show of great pattern art, such as the Matisse cutouts, which also included some slides projected on myself to show the students how I would look wearing them. During the period, I went from student to student modeling the most unusual outfits students created for me with the free-rolling tracing wheel and by stamping and stenciling designs on student-made fabrics.

My last example of a performance is from a lesson I called "Drawing from Significant Shared Experiences (Artists Respond and Comment on Life's Events)."

Most of the room lights were off and a tape-recorder loop was replaying a recording of the Space Shuttle *Challenger*'s brief journey. Chairs were randomly arranged in the room and the desks pushed in to the background. As students entered, they heard the countdown and the events of the shuttle disaster. The teacher was seated on the floor, surrounded by three chairs positioned as a space vehicle. "Tool boxes" were placed around the room—bright-red containers with art supplies in them (graphite powder and chalk dust in plastic pouches, torn sandpaper bits, metallic tapes, drawing tools tied to screwdrivers and pliers, foldout rulers). This box was labeled "Space Technicians Tool Kit." The teacher wore a motorcycle helmet with a NASA label.

The entering students were instructed to man their capsules, to sit inside their own chair designs, and, after the brief journey, to reenact the final destruction. The teacher explained that although the debris offered few clues, we can project possibilities and sketch the explosion. Students were asked, in drawing their reactions, to prepare the work surface as it would look if it had been damaged in flight and attach it to the largest section of the cabin remains.

Several quick drawings were made—some on silver foil, which a student decided would be a heat shield to be drawn on. Another student worked with what he called "a burning hot pencil," making impressions with it. Another student worked on torn bits of paper, as he said that it was "all that remained of the shuttle." Discussions during the experience centered on the possibility of using art to respond to special feelings, extraordinary events. We talked about the lasting qualities of art in making fleeting memories and momentary feelings more permanent.

4

Planning the Lesson

Just as the teaching of an art lesson is a creative performance, so planning the lesson is also an act of individual creativity. Creative lesson planning utilizes the individual teacher's artistic experience and insights. The best way to prepare for planning a lesson is to be fully productive as an artist, and to apply one's creative vision to lesson planning. When art teachers alter this vision to conform to the expectations of the school, the lessons they produce are stale and unfruitful. Only if teachers are models of the creative individual in their planning can they be models of the creative individual in their teaching.

Art is not (as students often assume) an unrestrained exploration in which anything and everything is acceptable in the name of self-expression: Intuition and emotional expression must be balanced by thought and planning. Artists are experienced planners. They know how to previsualize possibilities, to generate and sort through many options, to refine their approach to a problem, and to rehearse their artistic performance in order to perfect it. With senses finely tuned to the world around them, they are able to get ideas and develop them, building plans on an accumulation of experiences that can be returned to again and again. They can plan in the broadest terms, for they often carry an idea from work to work. The skills used to plan an artwork can be transferred to planning an art lesson: Designing the lesson can be viewed as making a work of art.

There is no one correct method of lesson planning. Each teacher needs to find the method of planning that works best for him or her. The source of lesson ideas is our own artistic experience, so part of planning involves reevaluating our creative ideas, sorting through them to determine what ideas will really challenge our students and what ways of presenting these ideas will be the clearest and most exciting. In planning, we question ourselves, our art—everything we have learned—and face a fundamental question: What about art is important to teach our students? The ideas we select should be both familiar and challenging—ideas that we have worked with and thought about extensively but that we still feel great interest in. They should be ideas that are based on our most interesting experiences and inspiring artistic visions.

Art lesson ideas derive from the art teacher's interests. Yet, as artist-teachers, we derive our ideas not only from the contemporary world in general but from our unique situation of being observers of children's artworks and of children's interests. Being with children presents an environment in which art teachers, as constant observers of children, develop a range of ideas for their teaching and their own artwork. Children present to the art teacher a unique view of the contemporary world and its possibilities for art. It is also a fact that artists gather their ideas from colleagues, other contemporary artists. Children are both contemporary artists and a unique group of colleagues who can inspire the art teacher.

A great deal of lesson planning, then, takes place years or months before the lesson is taught, while we are leading ordinary lives—gathering visual experiences, planning and making artworks, discussing art ideas with others, and, in general, exploring our own artistic vision. Lesson ideas may come to us at any time, and I have found it useful to keep "visual lesson-planning books"—sketchbooks and idea books in which I record lesson ideas. These are useful resources when the time arrives to do the final planning for the lesson.

At this stage of preliminary planning, the lesson plan can take many different forms. A great deal of planning may not appear on paper but may exist only in the artist's vision. How much each teacher needs to commit to paper varies. Some artists are more conceptual and some more intuitive. Some perform better with carefully documented plans, and some with little visible planning. Plans can consist of sketches, drawings, brief or lengthy written notes, collections, or clippings. Sketchbooks generally kept by artists and lesson ideas can be kept together for cross-fertilization. Usually notes help to visualize what the lesson may look like while writing assists the visual brainstorming process. Some documentation may exist only in the artist's mind; many artists are able to previsualize complex plans in detail and see them clearly without writing them down. It may, in fact, distort their ideas to put them down on paper. For such artists, when the standard lesson plan is used, vision is transformed into jargon, inspiration into formula, and the act of planning is no longer a creative enterprise.

Creative planning should lead to written lesson plans. The written school plan can be a useful reminder, a summary to oneself and others

*Paintings on wallpapers, suggested by lessons
exploring new canvas possibilities.*

of the many steps before it. The artist's planning should be the model for the artist-teacher's planning, which bears little resemblance to lessons planned the night before class. Artistic plans are the proud works of an artist, as the lesson should be the proud work of an art teacher. The idea books that contain lesson possibilities develop confidence and enthusiasm for the lesson.

Lesson plans are the fruit of our experience as artists. They have to ripen—to be built slowly, as art experiences and observations provide confirmation of the basic concept. Noting them down in a "plan" is simply the decision to put into effect lesson ideas that one has thought about for a long time.

Whatever the planning format, it is important to remember that the teacher's plans are designed to inspire the student's own planning. A written plan should not prescribe the art, but merely be an inspiration or guide the teacher's initial presentation. Teachers need the freedom to allow students to move away from plans and develop their own. Having written plans sometimes makes it difficult to allow others to move away from them. The art in a class comes from the responses, alterations, and explorations in response to the plan, not all of which can be written down or predicted.

SELECTING THE IDEA FOR THE LESSON

In planning a lesson, we do not start with a process or technique but with an idea—an idea that cuts across all the boundaries in art. This idea is the essence of the art lesson, and it must be communicated during the lesson in its simplest, most basic form.

In designing a lesson, we are attempting to build structures, major concepts on which students can base individual perceptions; we do not want to focus narrowly on the skills of a single technique. We all know ten typical school projects used to illustrate given techniques. We need to go beyond such projects to find for ourselves what we consider inspiring about a particular aspect of art and how to present it in a manner that inspires our students. We need to think inventively and globally. It is the richness and breadth of our presentation that will open up possibilities for the students. If we are able to select what is significant about art, so can they.

If stated simply, an idea can be built on richly. We can generalize from it broadly and generously, providing numerous examples from different media, artists, and periods in art history. For instance, we can define the essence of print making as the discovery, appreciation, and creation of beautiful surfaces; students can then extend the notion of what can be printed, finding new processes and new surfaces. But if we start with a study of the complex print-making process, vocabulary, and technique, students cannot begin to appreciate the basic notion of printing, or the idea of beautiful surfaces. They cannot easily build from these foundations.

To make sure that the lesson idea is clear, it is often valuable to state the objective of the lesson in words, using simple language and avoiding jargon. The objective must first speak to its designer, guiding him or her through the formulation of a lesson; only then will it be clear to the students to whom it is addressed.

In conceptual terms, the goal of the lesson is to present an art idea clearly and to help students learn how to relate different art ideas—to think analytically about art. Several planning strategies can help us to meet this goal. First, for any given idea we can try to present students with a wide range of examples drawn from the environment. If we are exploring a material such as plastic, for example, we can illustrate its use in contrasting objects—name tags, shrink wrappings, containers. If we are exploring the concept of reproduction, we can use tracings, stencils, carbon paper, photocopies, and rubbings. The variety of examples shows students how such basic ideas can be extended through environmental search and how to relate subcategories to the major concept.

Examples should be varied in terms of style and period. In a lesson on caricature, for example, we could use Disney cartoons, a court reporter's sketchbook, Hirshfeld's theatrical albums, Zen calligraphic portraits, and Calder's wire sculptures as illustrations. Children could engage in a variety of activities: They could make funny faces in a mirror and draw them on its surface, make graffiti on faces of newspaper advertisements, or sketch facial images over a video screen, to see the wide range of possibilities in characterizing the human face. Such contrasting examples help students grasp the broad meaning and the wide application of the art idea.

Comparisons and contrasts also help to clarify art ideas. We can plan to compare different artists and different works of art with each other or with the students' art, in terms of ideas, formats, materials, or other features. We can point out the relationships between the elements of an artwork and natural or designed environmental forms. For example, we could show how the human body takes on new meaning when it is studied as a sculptural form, a designed object, or a moving structure in space. Of course, contrasting ideas is as important as recognizing similarities among them. Contrasting geometric, hard-edged paintings with the work of abstract expressionists can stimulate the imagination. Showing contrasting views to students is a reminder to them that there is no single path but many solutions.

The conceptual structure of the lesson not only introduces students to significant art ideas; by illustrating the relationships among art ideas, the lesson also helps students learn to think about art analytically.

In addition, each plan needs to develop experiences that inspire visions, movements, and creative thoughts. It is to be a license to investigate and play out ideas. Each lesson plan is to become an example of artistic planning or the preparation of artists for making art. Each presentation is to display the question of what art is and what it could be, using the best visual examples to be found.

SELECTING THE PLAY IDEA

The main play idea for a lesson should be a kind of play that children already do. The teacher can plan to extend and adapt their play to art making, once he or she has learned it from the children. Like the art idea for the lesson, the main play idea for the lesson must be broad enough so that it can be elaborated in various ways and so that a variety of types of basic play can be used during the lesson. For example, "playing doctor" would be too narrow if it were treated as just a matter of doing the things doctors usually do (i.e., as a way of learning about medicine) but is fine when it is treated as a matter of exploring the art potential of a variety of things in the hospital environment such as clothing, paper, drawing tools, and so on.

The broad play idea for the lesson is always an imaginative, "make-believe" idea. Even if the inspiration is a real episode such as a visit to the hospital, in the classroom it can become make-believe, as in playing doctor. Why is this so? Perhaps because it is the easiest way to inspire students to want to try out the various kinds of play and art activities. Children can be inspired when they are taken places and put into exciting circumstances, such as going to the circus. Since, obviously, this can seldom be done with an entire class, fiction can be used instead to transform the classroom experience into something different and exciting. Since kids love to pretend, using an imaginative idea helps to put them into a free and creative frame of mind so that they can use their imaginations as they do when playing on their own. The teacher's use of imagination shows the children that imagination is wanted and valued in the art class. The goal of my art lessons is to make play and art making inseparable—one experience. I have found that almost any play idea can be adapted for art teaching, and many of the ordinary forms of play that children enjoy—block building or sand/water plays, for example—are in themselves forms of art play.

VISUAL LESSON PLANNING

Once the lesson idea has been selected, the teacher has to consider how to make the lesson visible. In other words, what will the lesson *look* like? At this stage we turn from examining the lesson idea analytically to view it imaginatively and poetically. Our purpose now is to translate the words that define the lesson's objectives into visual images that will bring the art idea alive and inspire the students. Visual notes are often helpful at this stage. Like the notes of designers, choreographers, and other artists who plan visual communications, the teacher's visual notes, in the form of sketches or diagrams, are not only an efficient means of gathering ideas but a way of probing the imagination deeply, to uncover old images and associations and create new ones.

In making visual plans, we should use sketchbooks, interesting drawing paper, colored pens—the materials we would use in planning our own artworks. Many visual ideas can be taken from the visual lesson-planning books we have kept, since these record the sights and experiences that initially interested us in the ideas and our developing thoughts about them. We will want to plan to bring some of the objects that originally inspired us along, to show students the sources of the lesson idea, displaying the finds from shopping trips (tools, materials, designed forms), the natural objects, the books and artworks that we learned from. We will also want to keep in mind the various visual aspects of the lesson, visualizing possibilities for classroom design, material design, displays, play activities, and the teacher's own performance. We can ask ourselves, what will the room look like? What colors, shapes, and movements will be seen? What sounds will be heard—will there be music? Will the room be dark or light; if light, will the light be "white" or colored? What fantasy ideas might be discussed or acted out? What will be the dominant materials, and what play activities do these suggest? What beautiful objects will be seen? What kind of performance do we ourselves want to give—subtle, humorous, or dramatic—or a dance? Would costumes help to show students images we want them to see? Should we or the children dance out images? What sort of stage design and props would we need?

What sort of colors, surfaces, and spaces will be used during the lesson, and how might these affect the students' art making and the end products? Will we use slides, films, or videos? Can we make use of the large surfaces of the room—the walls, ceiling, or windows? Do we want to stay entirely within the room or use the corridor or the lawn? How will we make our entrance? What will be the most surprising, dramatic, or humorous events planned for the lesson, and when will they occur? What kind of meaningful ending for the lesson can we envision?

At this initial stage of visualization, we are ranging freely among various images. We do not want to narrow our choices too quickly, before we have discovered our most inventive ideas and most deeply felt images. Sketching and drawing will help us sort through the various possibilities, to see which are the most interesting. It may not be clear yet, for example, whether, for this particular lesson, movement or color will be primary; whether the examination of significant displays, a performance by the teacher, or inventive play with unusual materials will be the central event of the class. The important thing is to run through in our minds the various categories of classroom experiences that could be used and to select the ones that present us with the strongest images, those that will work well together and will give the right emphasis.

Obviously we will be limited in some ways. We may have very little money to spend for materials, props, or costumes. The size or shape of the classroom may make it impossible to present certain types of performances or activities. If it is not a permanent art room, we may have to choose designs that make cleanup easy. We have to be sure that the lesson elements we select are compatible with one another. The room design must not conflict with movement plans or art making or interfere with sight lines, making it impossible for students to see a performance or demonstration. A favorite costume cannot be worn if it contradicts a color scheme asserted in the rest of the lesson. Such limitations are likely to seem minor, however, in comparison with the wealth of ideas that teachers can visualize for any given lesson once they become experienced in visual teaching. Often we can imagine more activities we would like to use, in numerous different combinations, than we will have time to present. The best can be saved to use in other lessons.

In making the final choices, we need to keep in mind that in art lessons, as in artworks, simplicity of statement and execution create the richest response. Using too many images or activities can make the presentation confusing. The introduction into the classroom of a single beautiful object or color, or a simple change in spatial arrangement,

Study of children's improvisations
in the sandbox, painted with gloves.

can be as dramatic and instructive as an elaborately staged performance. We need to choose the images and events that we think will convey the lesson idea most economically and clearly.

When the final selection has been made, we may want to note down our plan in a definitive form, making finished sketches and diagrams or written notes. I use word sheets (rather than complicated outlines) to remind myself of the relationships of ideas and images that I will explore during the lesson. Using a separate page for each group, I put the central idea or image in the middle of the page, arranging the related ideas or images around it. Whatever form of notation helps the individual teacher to formulate visual plans clearly is the form that should be used.

Considerations before an art lesson are similar to those of an artist thinking of an exhibit. Will the envisioned lesson be beautiful? Will it be exciting to experience and participate in? Will it be surprising and present something new? Will it challenge the viewer and hold his or her interest?

SOURCES OF LESSON IDEAS

Play Sources

At the 1987 National Art Education Association Convention in Boston, I invited my daughter, Ilona, a Suzuki music student, to play her violin. After her performance, I began my presentation with a familiar phrase of hers, "Dad, please don't forget to tell your students that this was my idea." Before proceeding any further with the meeting, I underscored her statement by saying, "Ilona wants you to know that these were all her ideas." (I paused.)

"My name is George Szekely. You may have seen me at our Atlanta meeting. I was the one rushing up the stairs clutching a collection of teddy bears under my arm. Or, maybe we bumped into each other in Chicago, where I recall the bellhop had a difficult time fitting all my skateboards and hoola hoops inside the hotel's glass elevators. Perhaps we met at the New York Hilton the year before and you may have seen my magician's suit and the red wagon I pulled, loaded with silver balloons and canisters of Legos and Day-Glo confetti. The reception was excellent at every event, with supportive comments such as, 'Professor Szekely, you have such wonderful ideas.'"

"You may know one of my colleagues who curiously peeks into my artroom. Oh, there goes Dr. Szekely under the tables, surrounded by windup toys and robots blowing amazing bubble shapes. That's Szekely, they shrug their shoulders. He's some sort of modern artist with strange ideas."

"Perhaps you were a student in one of my classes and you still have one of my Garbage Pail cards (by the way, I would appreciate if you would return them with my pickup sticks). Also, thanks for your teacher evaluations in telling me that I have great ideas."

At this point, I turned to my audience with the promise to let them in on my secret. "If you promise never to repeat this to anyone [and they swore to secrecy], I will share my secret with you." I continued then with a repetition of my introductory remark, "It was all Ilona's idea." Yes, it was Ilona's and many other children's ideas that for the past eighteen years I have observed closely and valued sufficiently to be brought to school. I find it interesting that these children's ideas and interests, their world, are not recognized when brought to school, and in fact, appear strange to my adult colleagues.

Significant art derives from any artist's deep concerns and interests. The child artist deals with interests that may be transformers, Barbie dolls, G. I.-Joe figures, or any number of play setups. The children's world often has little to do with the art interests of the teacher or the concerns of the art world. Art at home exists in exciting forms and is created with media that are not formal art supplies, or as a response to adult art problems and even without the presence of an art teacher. My concern has been to recognize children's interests and to import them to schools and conventions where they have not been welcomed before. We "play house" at the university and recognize all forms of children's play as the basis for school art. This children's play, however, exists at home and it is there that it needs immediate appreciation. The materials, props, and even playful thoughts commonly associated with children's interests are routinely kept out of school, considered to be distractions to learning. Children's play, toys, and inventions have been separated from school for so long that when they appear in a class, their values are difficult to recognize. Parents find it hard to recognize home art since it is so closely tied to children's playful actions, toys, and other such undervalued expressions.

Imagine the first slide of my presentation, which is a full view of a child's room after a typical day. It looks like it was hit by a storm or perhaps an earthquake. Each of the following slides explores closeups of the same room, demonstrating that after careful viewing, the space abounds in creative inventions. To an unsympathetic eye, it only looks like a messy room, one which most parents constantly fight to get cleaned up. On the other hand, the setup of dolls under a circular table is masterfully arranged with marbles and playing cards in between, demonstrating a sense of design rivaling the finest sculpture or painting. Another slide depicts a pink bubble-gum drawing effectively laid out on the side of a black garbarge can. The next slide reveals costume jewelry and clothespins displayed in the back of a toy truck. The last photograph is of our Sunday newspaper on the floor with a color treated front page, its black and white photographs retouched with nail polish and eyebrow pencils. The slides are examples of home art and children's inventions. This is contemporary art performed by modern artists utilizing new media, techniques, and surfaces that even the most avant garde adult artists have yet to examine. Environmental forms are freely used and a range of new media explored which only children playing naturally at home could discover. Art schools lag far behind in their traditional courses and media-divided classes, having yet to offer workshops in the printing of toy car tires on freshly painted walls or how to use Correct-type or toothpaste on a family checkbook. Art begins at home and may survive in its most exciting manifestations when sensitively supported and encouraged in its many unusual actions.

If you could see me pacing at home, in search of ideas before a class, you would also hear my daughter saying, "Dad, you look like you need a lesson." She confidently and seriously tells me, "Don't worry, I have one for you." This often includes her showing me something she is doing, a play work that I am made to promise will be shared with my classes. My daughter Ana, who is only four, has become aware of my interests as she shows me her nails to which she has pasted colored stickers and asks me, "Do you want to show me to your class?"

My teaching has been transformed as a result of taking seriously home artists. As lessons have become inspired by home art, I explain my finds and demonstrate how the ideas came about. The recipients of my instruction feel comfortable with the tools, sources, and ideas that are familiar and with which they have experimented. When I discuss lesson ideas with my children at home, it becomes a natural preparation for similar discussions at school. In other words, children's discoveries "play well" with other children. School art becomes child tested when it is an extension of home art. When art is based on the child's interest, it is approached with far greater commitment. The presentation of home art ideas and the utilization of their materials and media help to convince children that art is not a mysterious subject to which only adults have access, and that art ideas, indeed, can come from children. Home art deals with children's discoveries, improvisations, experiments, and ideas that school art can discover and build upon. The "new" in art may derive from discoveries and inventions by children at home as they turn tools and materials toward creative uses. Children are constantly engaged in adaptations of the environment and all its resources, few of which are recognized as "official" art supplies or artworks. The existence and creative uses of scented stickers, "magic" sand, or Day-Glo confetti are often discovered by the children first before they are even heard of by parents and teachers. Parents can't wait to give away children's toys. "When will the day finally come when the children will be more serious and stop playing?" "Your room is always a mess—when will you stop collecting all that junk?" "You can't bring all that stuff to school and you can't keep it at home either." "Just set the table and don't be so creative about it." Miraculously, in spite of thoughts and comments like these, home inventions often survive through play and home tasks. Home art is often viewed as wasteful play and its novel media and technical inventions frequently go unrecognized. Everyday chores and responsibilities often downplay these more valuable activities as mere annoyances and wastes of time. Yet, when we consider the great inventions by children that thrive in homes where creative ideas are welcome, we begin to appreciate our very own home artists.

Art experiences at home may derive from ideas generated through blowing bubbles, playing hopscotch, "house," or cat's cradle. Children create preliminary art ideas through informal playing, commonly referred to as creating "setups." Setups can be dolls or robots arranged about a circular table's legs with stickers and pictures posted around the table. Setups also utilize household objects, found "treasures," or toys with which children invent arrangements. Through photographic studies of setups and the study of children's sketchbooks that they kept at home, I found these creations to be rehearsals for artworks in which themes and design ideas are explored. It is important, therefore, for parents and teachers to pay attention to children's play and to recognize valuable means of formulating art ideas within it. Art teaching, in this regard, is the discovery of play ideas and how they can be followed up and expanded upon through art works.

Everything in the home is an opportunity for arrangements and display. Art ideas are discovered and played out through daily arrangement opportunities. Creativity is practiced through the child's ability to touch, select, move things about, and design with objects. As art on a canvas is the display and arrangement of lines and shapes, and sculpture is a composition of forms and movements, so are home tasks possibilities for two- and three-dimensional performances. Designs in the home may include formal displays in a living room showcase or settings of furniture in a playroom. Or they may be informal arrangements using different containers as "canvasses," such as the placements of clothing in a closet, shoes on a shelf, food in a refrigerator, or lunch in a lunchbox. Parents and children can focus on their artistic selves by noting personal arrangements and the organization of spaces and surfaces by each family member. The way lettering and words are organized on a postcard is a clue to the artistic display of a family member. Children can be encouraged to play with the way they set a table, hang up towels on a rack, or put their socks away. In being able to move things about freely and notice how household tasks have artistic possibilities, young children begin to freely design with pots and pans at an early age and then continue with many other media as they get older. Organizing and displaying plants around the room, dolls on a shelf, leaf piles in a yard, or food on a plate may receive special attention as design problems and solutions. Identifying home tasks as design problems, discussing them as artistic solutions, and challenging children to think of extensions of these in art media are significant contributions to art at home. Photographing, sketching, and discussing home arrangements and displays is most helpful. Play with toys that allow structuring, such as Legos, blocks, Brillo, marshmallows, or books, offers architectural learnings. When a child helps to place groceries in the refrigerator, not only the willingness to help should be noted, but the resulting displays admired and discussed as an artwork.

Listed below is a sampling of contemporary art and ideas discovered by children working at home. (Starred items are not officially sanctioned by parents.)

Mixing fruit yogurt as a color experience in painting
Drawing with different colored bubble gums
Lipstick prints on soft surfaces
Strawberry Nestle's Quik paintings on styrofoam plates
Nails as mini-canvases for sparkling nail polishes
Shoelaces to be worn with painted sneakers
Table settings with snow, spinach leaves, and Legos
Band-aid arrangements on skin
Sun-melted crayons on broken brick pieces
Pick-up stick arrangements
Moss and paint peelings in plastic bags
Sculptural bites in chips and apples
Graffiti works on the Sunday paper*
Drawing with toy car tires on freshly painted walls*

Kool-aid staining on rugs*
Drawings with jump ropes in the air
Musical scores with mixers and blenders
Drawing with a lawn mower on a field of grass
Drawing with a water hose while standing on a ladder
Ice cube sculptures in a sink

Home provides outstanding opportunities for artworks that may not look like art or be the products of traditional materials or processes. To find home art, we need to look beyond traditional boundaries and consider it as a truly contemporary medium speaking through environmental materials that reflect children's play concerns and interests.

Environmental Sources

Interesting lesson ideas are acquired only through experience, through the constant collecting of ideas from the visual world. Gathering lesson ideas is a full-time job. Planning, for both the artist and the art teacher, means being continually aware of the world around us. When planning is approached as a Sunday-night exercise, with the hope that inspiration will come, the lessons are generally uninspired and repetitive. The things that inspire us to make art can inspire lesson ideas: the visual environment (including both natural and designed objects), works of art, personal experiences, and so forth. Therefore the kind of research that is most important for art teaching is done not in a library but in the ordinary surroundings of everyday life. An hour or two spent in a toy store can be of much more use than studying a teaching manual.

Environmental search is as important for us as for our students. A visit to a shopping mall or supermarket, because it focuses our attention on immediate experience, can be an excellent source of lesson ideas. When we "shop" as teachers, we try to see beyond the ordinary uses of everyday objects and imagine new ways of responding to them. If we come upon an interesting assortment of work gloves, for example, we need to look beyond the expected uses of a glove and think of how we could use "glovelike qualities" for art making. A glove could be thought of as (1) a tool for painting, creating an original painting process; (2) a surface to paint on, as if the gloves were soft, shaped canvases; (3) a material resource to work with (medical, hunting, fire-fighting gloves, and so forth, use unusual leather, fabrics, and plastics); (4) an inspiration for other sculptural forms, since the gloves, with their different scales, materials, and textures, can be stuffed, made two-dimensional, serialized, exaggerated, abstracted, or given a new meaning, becoming a human form or an imaginary animal; or (5) a part of a new set of ideas, for instance, one that relates a glove to other coverings of the human form or to other sculptural clothing designs. The possibilities are endless. The most ordinary object can have innovative uses in art lessons: Rolling pins, notary sealers, and label makers can be used for printing; sewing machines, typewriters, erasers, pick-up sticks, and flashlights can be used for drawing.

In searching for materials and tools, we sometimes know what we will need for the lesson, but at other times we may let the objects themselves suggest lesson ideas. The search may be focused in various ways. For example, we can consciously investigate a variety of stores to find interesting materials and imagine how to adapt them for art making, regardless of their intended purpose. We can investigate the qualities of the materials to see how they can be used—new ways of draping, rolling, hanging, or folding foil or cloth, for instance, may be suggested by the texture, pattern, or surface of these materials. We can consider the qualities of traditional art materials and then consciously seek these in nontraditional materials—for example, using scrubbing tools, rollers, and sponges as brushes, or pegboards or cookie sheets as surfaces to paint on. We can focus on the tools and materials used in various professions, to see whether they can be adapted for art, borrowing the tracing paper, rulers, and marking tools of architects or fashion designers or the mixers, blenders, pastry bags, feather brushes, and spray frostings of the cake decorator.

By looking for art supplies ourselves, in the local community, we have a much more meaningful experience than when shopping is done through the traditional once-a-year ordering from a school-supply catalog—and we also save money. By purchasing supplies locally, at flea-markets and ordinary stores, at auctions and the supermarket, rather than through art-supply stores, we not only are exposed to a much wider variety of possibilities to choose from but, by utilizing nontraditional supplies, can often get things more cheaply. Instead of spending all our money in advance at one time, having money on hand enables us to make our own finds and bring them to class while we still feel the excitement of discovery and can convey it to the children, whom we are teaching to be shoppers themselves.

We can also do creative shopping inside the school, where we can get many materials for nothing. Instead of buying pickup sticks to dip into drawing ink, for example, we can use straws from the cafeteria.

The school office may be able to give us interesting folders, labels, fastening materials, and envelopes, used or new, for drawing surfaces. Shop teachers can give us wood and other scraps. If large objects such as computers are purchased for the school, the "trash" or wrapping materials may become a treasure for us. In just looking around the classroom, we can find all sorts of things to use—books for building blocks, or children's umbrellas for constructing cities of the future.

We can also shop for lesson ideas by looking through catalogs. They present countless new designed forms, in a manageable format, and show us the latest designs in a wide variety of objects. Each catalog is a vast resource of forms, subjects, colors, patterns, and sculptural shapes. Catalogs present many possible forms of the same objects, allowing us to compare and select. Since the images in catalogs are merely small, flat, abstract symbols of objects, catalogs provide perspective, helping us to reinterpret the forms displayed in them, so that we may see hand tools as beautiful shapes for sculpting, tents as shaped canvases, or the quilted fabric of a ski jacket as a surface that, bought by the yard, we would like to paint on.

Television has given today's children, the "television generation," a unique exposure to sophisticated visual experiences. Such experiences are reflected in children's art and have enormous potential for art teaching. A television-trained child with a powerful remote-control device in his or her hand becomes a junior cameraperson who already knows a great deal about such things as animation and set design. The children of today have been exposed to a vast array of images, including a great variety of architecture and interiors, and are also constantly seeing, through advertising, the latest in fashion and product designs. To them, some extremely sophisticated extensions to ordinary ways of seeing that were unknown to prefilm generations—slow motion, instant replay, computerized graphics, instant closeups—are familiar experiences. Television images and techniques can provide art teachers with inspiration for unusual drawing exercises, new ways of viewing one's own art, videotape and multimedia art making, and many other learning activities. Although television has long been accepted as an educational tool in the schools, we have only begun to explore its potential for art teaching.

Many artists enjoy television immensely. To them it represents both the ultimate realism (in its wealth of naturalistic images) and the ultimate illusion, because it employs all of the techniques of illusion, such as lighting, perspective, and shading, that we use in art. One of the purposes of exploring television with our students can be to help them move away from mindless viewing to an appreciation of the uniqueness of television: in other words, to appreciate television as artists do.

The most obvious influence of television on children's art is seen in their selection of TV heroes for their art—cartoon characters, detectives, and even characters from commercials. Their drawings of such characters are done in television "space," with the figures displayed as though on a paper "screen." At every age, children make a great effort to draw the kinds of actions and moving figures, and even the colors, that they are familiar with from television. Our children are accustomed to looking at the world through the television-screen window. Much of their art is an interpretation of seeing "through" the TV screen, as John Nagy, the noted television art teacher, emphasized by encouraging children to color images directly on plastic lenses placed directly over the television screen.

It is not difficult to invent new ways to use television that promote more active viewing and encourage students to adapt television experiences and techniques for their own art making. For example, we can encourage children to watch TV without the sound; to trace colors or lines from the screen; to play with the controls, to increase the contrast, or change the color; to compare the images on a black-and-white TV with those on a color screen next to it that is set to the same channel; to compare the images on a small and a large screen; or to observe the sequence of images made by playing with remote-control devices. As with other types of observation, active viewing can be encouraged through creative talking about what is viewed and by having students take notes on visual ideas for their sketchbooks. The video camera can be used as an art tool for probing one's own artwork or focusing on the environment, storing visual images and memories. It is also a powerful sketching tool, allowing ideas to be shopped for, saved, and recalled for later use. Students can also videotape evaluations of their artwork as "TV shows" to be presented to the class, which provides the students who produce the shows with firsthand experience in television filmmaking (some examples are given later in Chapter 5). As one of the most powerful visual influences on children today, television can be a valuable aid to art teaching, where it can serve as a unique bridge between children's interests and the world of art.

Another way to learn what inspires children visually is to familiarize ourselves with illustrated children's books, both old and new. The many beautifully illustrated books available for younger children can be used as part of a lesson, or given to an individual child as a resource for his or her planning. Many children already enjoy such books, eagerly entering into the imaginative experiences of the stories. By calling their attention to the illustrations, rather than stressing the text as is usually done in school, we can help them to make creative use of the visual experience the books provide. More recent children's books with innovative formats—parts that fold out, pop up, or require assembly; new play forms that straddle the boundary between books and sculptural objects to be used in play (books with wheels, books that make sounds, books that talk or require special viewing devices, books printed on three-dimensional forms); and book packages that include tapes, records, slides, or other visuals may be used in a lesson or may inspire lesson ideas.

TIMING AND SEQUENCING

In all performance arts, including teaching, the timing and sequencing of the performance is an art form in itself. This aspect of the lesson requires careful planning if the lesson is to be effective.

The standard art lesson follows a conventional sequence of activities. It is divided into three parts: the introduction, in which the teacher presents the lesson ideas and gives instructions; the body of the lesson, in which the students work, carrying out the teacher's instructions; and the end, which is devoted to review, cleanup, and evaluation of work. As we have seen, the constituent elements of an innovative art lesson are quite different from this: Instruction is carried out in many ways besides lecturing; students are learning before, during, and after the art making; much more time is spent on planning and preparation; and evaluation occurs during the art making as well as after. Whatever activities we are working with, though, we should try to avoid falling into a routine sequence. Although students should become familiar with certain types of activity that are new to them, such as experimental play with art materials, movement exercises, or viewing a performance by the teacher, the essence of art is the unexpected. Students should come to class feeling that they never know exactly what kinds of things will happen, or in what order.

A class period can be envisioned as a series of quick play episodes with pauses in between during which students take notes on the ideas and discoveries they found through the play. I sometimes develop a series of fast exercises involving physical activity that last throughout the period. Each session involves quick play with materials, props, or the environment. For example, one segment may deal with folding, another with crushing, draping, or wrapping a particular material.

Rather than envisioning a lesson as consisting of a brief teacher introduction and a long student work period, student play can be introduced into the lesson at any point. Play can initiate or inspire an
artwork, or used to study a completed artwork—by examining it with
a flashlight, looking at it through a funnel, or going over it with a
magnifying glass. In this case, a completed artwork is used as a playful
beginning to start a lesson. Visual inspirations, or a show-and-tell
session about beautiful objects, can also be introduced at any point
during the lesson. Here again an art lesson can start with completed
works and involve the generation of new plans and ideas from them.

Finally, lessons can begin with the students' performance and play
or with a teacher presentation. These can be visual or verbal. Rather
than planning for the introduction to a lesson, as most art teachers do,
we need to think about the flow of the lesson as displays are changed,
materials and work areas are varied, and students move from exploring one technique to another.

A lesson can also be viewed as alternating between times in which
students are physically active, as when they are playing or making art,
and more contemplative, quieter times when they are listening, observing, and contemplating. Slow-paced activities, as we have noted
earlier, are needed, especially with young children, so that they can
observe and think about what they are doing instead of rushing to
finish their work. Pauses are also valuable and need to be planned for.
An artwork is made as much by thinking about it as by active, physical
work. Time spent sitting quietly in front of a work and looking at it, or
even walking around the room, is often useful, for it allows creative
contemplation of the work's possibilities. We adult artists take breaks
in just the same way when we make our own works. Instead of fearing
such pauses as disruptions of the lesson, we need to plan to build them
into the lesson and allow each student to work at his or her own pace.

Fast-paced activities are valuable for eliciting spontaneous responses. A rush of activity can be used to surprise students, helping
them break away from set patterns and familiar ways of doing things,
as when, for example, we try to help children draw more freely by
asking them to imagine that they can draw faster than anybody in the
world. A rapid pace can also produce a sense of pressure that forces
decisions, in contrast to a leisurely pace that allows more deliberate
consideration. The pace of the lesson can be varied, rather easily, by
the teacher's actions and gestures—either overtly, through the announcement of deadlines, quotas, or schedules, or more subtly,
through the speed of the teacher's movements and the quiet or excited
tone of the teacher's talk.

The timing and pacing of an art lesson are also affected by a much larger problem concerning time. School time is designed for subjects dispensing information and not for the self-paced search for ideas. The time allotted to art classes in the school curriculum is simply inadequate. Whereas other subjects are taught for a full period every day, art is sometimes scheduled as a Friday-afternoon activity in the lower grades. In the upper grades, one period is hardly enough for individual investigation, material handling, and cleanup. In response, art teachers tend to push students to work too fast and, in an effort to teach efficiently, may present art ideas in oversimplified form and themselves take over many of the important aspects of the art-making process from the student-artists. When this happens, we are allowing time constraints to prevent real learning about art in the classroom.

Instead of permitting ourselves and our students to be rushed by these time constraints into a faster pace of working than art realistically requires, our response must be to teach students how to manage their own time—how to use their class time well and to find the extra time that they need outside of class. The amount of time they will have later in life for art will never be enough either. If they learn well now, they will be able to balance the time pressures of the typical art lesson with the need for leisurely experimentation and slow-paced observation. They will exhibit patience and concentration, even in the fast-paced setting of the schoolroom. We ourselves must model this approach by refusing to be rushed in class and by building time for pauses, play, conversation about art, and evaluation of artworks into the lesson. We can also "stretch" the time by assigning students to do much of their learning outside of class.

The teacher must have the sequence of lessons for the term in mind well in advance and, during the term, will have to become skilled at keeping several balls in the air at the same time, using parts of many lesson periods to introduce ideas and make assignments for future lessons. The fact that assignments are given in advance is in itself a signal to students that artworks are not just made on the spur of the moment but require planning and preparation. By encouraging students to discuss the progress of their plans with others in the class whenever possible, class and teacher serve as an audience whose reactions can help to guide a work. In this way students learn that even the best plan is only a beginning requiring considerable refinement. Because, for a given lesson, all of the students will be working with the same broad lesson idea, we will have the coherence we need in order to provide guidance and suggestions, while leaving them plenty of room to make their own individual investigations.

Finally, teachers should plan lessons that can be continued for several sessions. Students will then have to think about art outside the classroom, preparing for each session by collecting ideas and considering the direction their work will take. Through this strategy, teachers will accomplish what is perhaps the most important aim of art instruction: making art not just a classroom activity but a part of the student's life.

PLANNING FOR INDEPENDENT WORK

Every aspect of the lesson is designed to encourage students to work independently. The lesson as a whole is designed to inspire students to take responsibility for their own work and to do a great deal of it on their own time, outside of class. The teacher, by behaving as mentor and model rather than authority figure, lets students know that they will make major decisions for their works themselves.

There are also specific points to keep in mind in planning for students to work independently. We want students to realize that art does not come into being instantaneously but that creative works, and ideas for works, are built slowly, over a period of time and through many works. Works and ideas need to be thought about and envisioned both in preparation for the work, *before* it is made, and *afterward*, in response to what has been created. No piece of art is ever necessarily finished; a "completed" work always suggests possibilities for new works and ideas that might follow it and also reflects thoughts and works that precede it. To experience this process of building ideas and works, students should often make works in series, one right after another, or make several sets or series of pieces at the same time rather than working on only one piece during a period. It is also quite all right to let several periods go by without having any artworks completed, since these lessons may have actually produced valuable plans and ideas that will eventually result in more meaningful works. Students also need to feel that artistic progression is something to be felt from within, not imposed by a teacher. They need to look at their own works-in-progress from a long-term perspective.

In choosing lesson ideas, teachers should not think of lessons and art projects as separate units that cannot be allowed to overlap. On the contrary, lessons should be designed to encourage students to return to earlier works and reexplore them, and to stay with and develop ideas and projects from early lessons that interest them. The goal is not to make sure that each student finishes a single work within each period or for each lesson: Art learning does not have this kind of simple linear progression. The goal is to make sure that students explore in depth whatever ideas and works they are dealing with and that they learn to build from one artistic experience to the next. By choosing for the subject of art lessons broad ideas that potentially include many media and techniques, we gain the flexibility that is needed to permit students to follow their ideas wherever they lead. By keeping the focus, as we plan, on the art process and on the interrelationships of art ideas and media, rather than on separate media and techniques, we will avoid boxing students into separate projects and lessons that prevent them from building on their art experiences. We will forget about the production-line idea of having each student produce one specific type of art project for every lesson and free our students to discover their individual directions and rates of progress.

Students need to be given long-term assignments if they are to plan their work. Assignments can be given days, weeks, or months in advance. Besides assigning specific categories for environmental search (as described in Chapter 2), we can make specific homework assignments in which students are asked to:

- Watch films, videotapes, and television shows relevant to the lesson. Also, record ideas for lessons on tape, film, and video as well as in sketchbooks.
- Play with simple materials specified for the lesson, to develop preliminary skills, ideas, and confidence, or find simple materials such as gum and toothpaste, to draw, paint, or arrange in exploring a lesson idea.
- Think about the problem the lesson poses.
- Write about the lesson problem and envision a variety of solutions. Create lists of ordinary solution ideas and a list of unusual ideas.
- Observe places and things related to the lesson. Visit a flea market or a supermarket with the eye of an artist, reviewing and collecting interesting finds related to the lesson.
- Talk about ideas for the lesson with a variety of people.
- Visit a library, museum, or gallery to study, looking for allies, heroes, and interests in all art fields, or for specific visual ideas for the lesson.
- Create preliminary sketches, diagrams, or artworks in preparation for the lesson.

- Seek a contemplative state and environment for artistic meditation such as taking a walk or a bike ride where the sole intent is to visualize and think about possibilities for a problem.
- Perform, act out, design events such as parties, plays, and skits to try out art ideas.
- Examine home chores as creative resources, finding in vacuuming or raking leaves some tools, movements, and processes that can relate to an art lesson.

Teaching students to use sketchbooks and other idea books is, of course, one of the most important ways of helping them to work independently, so getting them started on their sketchbooks is one of the things we must plan to do early in the term. The teacher should keep an eye out for trips or other special events that could provide good sketchbook material. To suggest the range of possibilities for student record books, here is a list of some of the types that we have used:

diary books, in which events and students' responses to them can be sketched

observation books, in which specific observations about space, light, or textures in the environment can be noted

big ideas books, for planning large artworks that will later be translated from the sketchbook to the appropriate medium

experimental (or doodle) books, for playful experiments with the sketchbook surface, using different materials and movements to discover intuitive art ideas

special trips books, in which a car trip, walking tour, or plane flight is recorded, along with the student's response to what he or she found most interesting about it

movement plan books, to choreograph movements to be used in a painting or sculpture, describing points in the artwork where one enters or exits, or how one crosses the stage or paper

future plan books, containing the students' lesson plans or steps to be taken in developing an artwork that the student has chosen to execute

media notebooks, which may be collections of photographs, tape recordings, or films of ideas that can be supplemented by a written or diagrammed sketchbook

environmental sampler books, which can include clippings, photos, brochures, and so forth, that may be inserted into an idea

book with written or diagrammed commentary or instructions
for one's own use

poetic observations books, for responses to feelings and observations through poetic language that can perhaps be translated
into drawings, paintings, or other artworks

theme books, in which a theme such as food or space or trees can
be elaborated.

We also need to seek opportunities to go over students' sketchbooks
with them regularly, so that we can help them to develop their ideas
and learn how to use the sketchbook to further their art.

Some teachers assume that the sheer numbers of students, as well as
limited storage and work space, make such independent work impossible. Individual plans require individual attention, plus individual materials and use of space. If students are eased into self-planning, however,
a different set of class rules and routines is slowly established. As
students become more responsible for planning their work, they become
more responsible in their attitudes as well. The teacher spends less time
on general instruction and discipline and has more time to spend helping
individuals. Storage problems decrease instead of increasing; when students work independently, they spend more time planning and concep-
tualizing artworks and often create more thoughtful and personal statements. This frequently means that fewer pieces are produced than when
each period yields an artwork from each student.

Students themselves often object to independent work at first.
Many of them feel insecure about working without explicit instructions, and they argue that planning is the teacher's job. Some are
shocked that the art teacher expects them to do homework. It is true
that the more structured the class, the more secure students feel, but if
students are to become artists, they must learn to deal with this inse-
curity. The uncertainty they feel in planning on their own is the
uncertainty that artists face every time they work. As for homework, it
is as necessary for art as for any other school subject, and if students
are enjoying their artistic work and their class experience, most of
them are willing to do some work outside of class. The level of home
preparation will vary, with some students doing less work at home
than others. Still, students need consistent praise and encouragement
for independent efforts and for items included in their idea sketchbooks that allow continuous planning and reference to work in class.

Keeping track of the progress of a student's work and keeping the
work moving, like other parts of art making, must become more the

student's responsibility than the teacher's. Art learning equires a steady seeking to understand one's own progress, an awareness of changes of direction and interest, and knowledge of the connection between works. This can be learned only by managing the development of a work, and the transitions between different works, oneself. Knowing what work needs to be done, which pieces are complete or need to be returned to, is an essential artistic task, an important part of taking responsibility for one's own art that needs to be discussed with students. Teaching students to manage their own progress is inseparable from teaching them to manage their own ideas. Managing a single work—deciding on its beginning(s) and conclusion(s)—is the first step in learning to manage a body of works, which also has many beginnings and conclusions.

Teachers are too often concerned with making sure that students complete individual works, counting the completed works, and grading them (which effectively "completes" the work, since after a work has been graded students leave the ideas embodied in it alone). Instead, our major emphasis must be on teaching students to evaluate their own works and be aware of their own progress. This can be done by examining with them the pieces they are working on, reviewing with them their idea books, and looking through their portfolios with them, helping them to evaluate their progress through conversation with the teacher. Instead of viewing unfinished works as a problem and worrying about having students complete them, we can see that they are a great learning tool for students to use, since they remind students of ideas they have had earlier and help them to develop new strategies. Students need to have the freedom to leave works unfinished, to take them out of class, to bring them back, to return to old works, to create several pieces simultaneously, and to live with unfinished works, since this is how artists build their work. An art portfolio is not a storage vault—although it is often used as one in school. Instead it should be an active file of incomplete works and completed works that can be examined and freely returned to as new works and experiences bring new insights.

PLANNING FOR DISCUSSIONS IN ART

I like to begin my classes by presenting my lesson ideas in the form of beautiful objects to see, new play activities, or a performance that I do. After that, the students talk, and their discussions in essence become their preparations or lesson plans for designing how they are going to utilize the initial inspiration and the possibilities it suggests. Talking before working is the essential ingredient that moves the lesson from what the teacher plans, performs, and exhibits to what the students want to do, making the result their own art.

Through discussions, art problems are stretched beyond their first impressions and ordinary reactions and are built toward extraordinary responses, unusual perceptions, and highly imaginative insights. Student talk allows expeditions beyond the classroom limits and permits art ideas to be boundless, as students dream of making prints from the bottom of the sea, snapshots of heaven, or rubbings of the pyramids. Talking, therefore, leads beyond first impressions, beyond teacher assignments, beyond school art, and stresses the importance of student ideas. Students also learn the important notion that art deals with ideas and is not simply making things, and that ideas they talk about may become artworks but can also stand as important creations in themselves.

Talking helps to build dedication to one's work. Students get truly excited about ideas they formulate. Through discussion, ideas are rehearsed and become clearer in the students' minds. In speaking to others, one is committed to an idea, to a challenge, and it thereby becomes more real and more possible to attain. Talking about the work helps to diminish anxiety and lets students focus on solutions, rather than just foreseeing problems. Discussing the work, therefore, actually helps to make it. Only a small part of an artwork is physical work, and as the details, steps, techniques, and materials are questioned through conversation and individually decided on, the artwork is actually being made.

In planning for conversations in art, we need to remember that students are primarily interested in learning things relevant to their own art. Conversations must therefore focus on the students' individual ideas and concerns, and not on general themes with which the students should supposedly be acquainted. We can easily build from students' concerns to broad art ideas and examples from other artists' works that are truly relevant and interesting, because they are mentioned not for their own sake but because they have bearing on what the students are thinking and doing.

Conversations can take place at any point during the lesson, either with groups or with individual students. The teacher does not pose as the "expert" in all matters but functions as a supportive colleague, a facilitator in finding out about artists and one's artist self. Apart from a student's own work, subjects that lend themselves to such discussions include:

- the teacher's sources and inspirations for the lesson;
- the relevance of the lesson to the works of other artists;
- the similarities or differences between student ideas and art-works and those of other artists;
- students' interpretations of and reactions to the lesson;
- students' evaluation of their own works in progress or of completed works;
- discoveries made by students during the art process, and problems they encountered;
- ideas for future artworks based on individual performance and assessment;
- what the teacher has learned from the experience.

STUDYING OTHER ARTISTS AND THE ART WORLD

Students need to understand that although they have an art teacher in school, they need to have many other teachers, to be apprenticed to other artists they themselves admire. When they leave school, they will need to have already developed the habit of looking for answers to art problems in the works of other artists who inspire them. Even young children can learn to look to artists such as Picasso or LaLique, Marcel Marceau or Yves St. Laurent, for color or line ideas; to compare their own approach to an art problem with the approach used by Antonio Gaudí, Maurice Sendak, or Russel Wright; to think about and discuss art ideas expressed by famous artists; and to consider the pragmatic aspects of art making, such as how a work can be exhibited, how artists budget their time, or how works can be stored. By planning to make such things a natural part of every art lesson, we teach children to draw their art ideas from the best sources, to measure their own art against the most up-to-date and most varied examples, and, ultimately, to think of themselves as artists, members of the art world. We demystify the art world and help children to see great artists as familiar and worthy models—people they can admire, identify with, and imitate.

As I noted in discussing classroom displays (in Chapter 2), examples of both past and contemporary artworks should be regularly used in lessons to establish comparisons between the children's projects and the works of professional artists. The contemporary artist is free to search and utilize ideas from all art forms, styles, and periods. Students as contemporary artists can be inspired by designers, dancers, painters, or crafts people. Assignments in which children visit museums or browse through art books can serve the same purpose. Besides becoming familiar with well-known artworks, children need to learn about artists' lives—their working methods, personal and professional problems and triumphs, personalities and social life, and above all, their ideas. We should introduce them to artists' writings and biographies, as well as their works.

I often begin a class, for example, by reading statements artists have made about their most significant art experiences—Atget's receiving his first camera, Kandinsky his first paint set; Matisse's feelings about copying an artwork exactly, Renoir's about the various models that inspired him. Students identify with the growth, the joy of discovery, represented by these statements, for they have had such experiences themselves.

Once we have shown the way by suggesting comparisons between students' art making and that of other artists, our students begin to make such comparisons on their own. Comparison yields numerous valuable insights. First, students see how different artists have handled the same problem: They see the many possibilities inherent in a single idea, the rich elaboration it allows. Not only does this show them that there are numerous solutions to a given problem; it tells them that their own approach, however unorthodox, is also valid. They see that there are many ways to handle an artwork and that it is important for them to search for their own solutions.

Students also learn more about the art-making process. They see how artists take what they observe and transform it into art; how they elaborate, simplify, or enlarge ideas; how they decide which materials, tools, and techniques to use; how they break through old habits to achieve a new way of seeing; how they take advantage of accidental discoveries; how they rework or remake works, deciding when and how finally to end them; how they deal with dissatisfaction, clarifying and refocusing ideas in additional works; and how they deal with audience response and criticism. They see how artists throughout the ages have handled the same problems they are now confronting. With the artist as model, students are able to assess their ideas as well as their skills; to grasp the perceptions, values, and commitments that go into creating a work of art; to find out what interests them by investigating a wide range of types of artistic expression; and to establish artistic goals of their own. Thus, by studying artists, students learn more than history or technique; they learn something that is personally meaningful to them.

ENDING THE LESSON

Planning the ending of the lesson is as important as planning the beginning. The ending of the lesson should be a time for reflecting on the artworks completed during the lesson or on the lesson experience itself. The ending can focus on the teacher's final statement, on independent evaluations by individual students, or on group activities.

Ending a work of art is a momentous decision for an artist. Some endings are smooth and predictable; others are mysterious and difficult, the result of considerable struggle and sudden inspiration. Certainly no two endings are ever the same. Yet, however a work is concluded, its conclusion is of great significance both for the individual work and for the artist's work as a whole.

When a work "feels" right, artists are filled with confidence and pride, able to visualize new possibilities and to take on new challenges. But the completion of a work can also be a time of conflicting emotions—satisfaction that the work is done, but confusion about what it has accomplished, or disappointment that it has not fulfilled the artist's original intentions. In any case, the artist must review the work, decide what can be learned from it, and move on to the next one.

Making art is a continuing process, with the artist seeking to develop ideas from one work to the next. Ending a work of art is thus only a temporary break, a time for reflection that inspires further ideas and further works. Artists assess what they have accomplished; they review their journey, so to speak. They see where departures have been made, and, because the final product can never match the original conception, they see what remains to be explored in the next project. Thus, the ending of a work is also a beginning, a time of preparation for new works. Each ending helps the artist build toward a larger vision that the ending has served to clarify.

Students in an art class need the challenge of ending a work as an artist does. The ending is an essential aspect of the art-making process, and the decision about when and how to end is one that only the artist can make. The ending must be envisioned, as inspired as was the beginning of the work. Yet in the classroom the completion of a work of art is seldom a significant moment. Indeed, school endings are generally uneventful, yielding little of the excitement and satisfaction yielded by other parts of the lesson. Most often, endings are not dictated by the works themselves but by the school bell. Completion of a work is rushed, with little time given the students to savor and assess their work. The emphasis is on quick cleanup, not on artistic concerns. And because students are assumed to have all worked at the same pace and to have solved the same artistic problem at the same time, students are not given the opportunity to explore ongoing artistic concerns outside the classroom.

Teachers seldom help students plan meaningful endings. In fact, they often unintentionally bring about inappropriate endings. On the one hand, they may praise a work so highly that a student then hesitates to add to it. On the other hand, they may encourage a student who wants to end a work before the period is over to continue working until the time is up, pointlessly adding to a work that is already complete.

Throughout the art-making process, the work keeps changing and evolving, presenting a continuous flow of possibilities. At some point, the artist needs to stop this flow of images and decide what the completed work is to look like. Ending a work is thus a matter of recognition, of choosing from the flow of images that the work generates, the one image that is appropriate, that suits the artist's needs and intentions. Thus, since to end a work is to arrest a changing visual statement, to interfere with a work's ending means changing the work.

Students must be given the opportunity to end their works for themselves. They must have the chance to assess their works, to deal with the elation, confusion, or disappointment of a particular ending, and to go on from there. They must be allowed to ask questions about their works, so that they begin to understand both the work they have just completed and the art-making process itself. Students must learn to see the ideas exhibited by a completed work and to build on these ideas, making the work a basis for new ones. They must learn to carry the art-making process outside the classroom, so that, inspired by what they have just completed, they can continue the art-making process by gathering and recording new ideas on their own.

Given the restraints of the classroom, how can a teacher keep from interfering with the ending of a student's work? How can students be given the time and opportunity to end their works as they see fit?

Artists cannot create all the time; life makes other demands upon them, and these demands must be met. Young artists in school are even more restricted, unable to work long without interruption because of class schedules. Poorly timed endings are thus hard to avoid. But the pace of the work *can* be allowed to vary. Indeed, it *should* be allowed to vary. The amount of time spent on a project should be dictated by the work. Flexibly timed endings—that is, allowing students to declare a work completed when they feel it is complete, regardless of lesson plan or the length of the period—are the best way to help students learn to end their works effectively.

Students should be free to work on several pieces at once, for one piece can suggest an ending for another. They should also be free to return to earlier works. This way, they can end a work without having to commit themselves to that ending. In fact, such "endings" are common for artists. A work may have several endings as the artist takes a break from it, goes on to other works, and then returns to it later. Students should have the same opportunity. Sometimes students return to older works not to revise them but to compare them with a work just completed. They can then trace the progress of an idea from work to work. They can see where one idea has come from, how it was developed, and how far it might be extended. They can see which works are temporary detours and which ones are important break-throughs. They may have to return to a particular piece again and again to determine its significance.

Students can review their works to assess their accomplishments in a number of ways. They can, for example, compare a finished work with the various stages through which it has passed, if the construction has been recorded on videotape.

Another way to review a newly completed work is to redraw it. I call such quick sketches "summary works." They allow students to visualize the various stages through which the work has passed, to see whether the original intention has been fulfilled, to assess unexpected developments, and to identify simply and directly the essential aspects of a work. Students can then review the work, acting as an audience, and can demonstrate a clear understanding of their creations without duplicating the struggle they went through to create them initially. (Any of the other techniques for evaluating art through art, described earlier, can also be used.)

Having students write creatively about their works often enhances their understanding of what they have accomplished. Poems and sto-ries focus students' attention on a work, helping them to organize their thoughts. By using another medium to describe a work's details and construction, students are able to express their feelings about their work. Not only may they feel reassured about what they have created, but they may get ideas for new works. By acting as an audience for their own works, students are able to attain a new level of perception and meaning.

If endings can inspire introspection, they can also inspire celebra-tion—the sharing of art with others. Just as artists celebrate their creations through gallery openings, fashion shows, and slide presenta-tions, so student artists should have the opportunity to present their works to an audience. At the same time, they will have the opportunity to see their work in new surroundings and be able to handle it, play with it, use it, and talk about it, rather than simply making and storing it. This type of ending gives children confidence not only in their art but in the presentation of it.

Celebrations can take numerous forms. Artworks can become performance pieces that talk, describing themselves and interacting with other works. Works can be used in performances as costumes, masks, puppets, or backdrops for production. Students can learn about a work by pretending to become that work, representing the movement it suggests and responding to its colors and how the work makes them feel. Games also promote students' responses. Taking the shape of a piece and walking like it or drawing a duplicate in the air, parading it, using it for show-and-tell, showing slides of it—these all make the child feel like an artist and encourage thoughtful reflection on a work.

Finally, role-playing activities allow students to respond to a work from different perspectives. Students can enact the role of critic, historian, gallery guide, curator, or artist's friend. They can act as audiences of different ages, cultures, or artistic persuasions. Role playing gives them the opportunity to envision playfully a variety of responses to their work.

If both student and teacher are excited by what they have learned during the lesson, both grow because of it; their thoughts are not the same at the end of class as they were at the beginning. Teachers should always try to sum up these thoughts in a final statement, and they should encourage students to sum up their thoughts as well. A teacher's final statement, when well planned, is among the most effective teaching tools. Because time at the end of class is short, the statement given must be clear and succinct, yet it must still be significant, encouraging students to consider the meaning of the experience they have just had and giving them insight into the art process and artistic thought. The statement can be a general one planned beforehand, or it may be inspired by specific works of art. It may be a performance, entailing the display of a review, poem, or quotations from artists that are relevant to the activity just completed. Although some final statements will be strictly verbal, others may be visual, consisting of images or objects that further inspire the students. The following categories are especially appropriate for end statements.

- *Wisdom handed down from one's own teachers, or stories and anecdotes about other artists.* Diane Arbus, the famous photographer, whom I also admired as my teacher, said that there is "always a gap between intention and effect." Something is ironic in the world, and it has to do with the fact that what you intend never comes out as you intend it to. (Diane Arbus, *Diane Arbus*. New York: Aperture Press, 1972, p. 2). In quoting Arbus, I am relating to students who were unhappy about their work and perhaps threw it into the trashcan. Even though we spend a great deal of time planning and thinking about our art, there also needs to be a feeling of letting go of those plans and to view art as an unpredictable journey. Since we cannot completely predict the outcome, we are often surprised by our own work, by its unfamiliar face that does not look like what we expected. I explain the necessity of learning from work that is different from what is expected and how, as an art teacher, even though I plan carefully, I always welcome surprises, which make my work exciting.

- *Picking up on observations or discoveries, or retracing what happened in class.* I may remind my students that before they wash their tables after painting, they should study the marks around the work. What remains *beside* the art paper has a great deal to say about the work, providing clues as to the choices, techniques, and movements used to make it. Some students notice a heavier emphasis, richer colors, or more notations on one side than another. Other students observe loose, runny edges or flowing color surrounding the piece. Cleanup time is observation time, and one need not be totally engrossed in routines. Shapes cut away from an art work, mixing trays, and all the remnants and tools used for making the work are part of it. We can learn from even the smallest clues.

- *Remarks designed to encourage useful work habits.* There are two important kinds of books in the life of a student artist that are symbolic of one's learning. One is a notebook, in which to take notes from workshops, classes, or teachers, recording remarks, the teachings of others. The other kind of books are our own idea books, where we take account of and seriously record our own ideas. It is important to take note of one's own ideas, to recognize that one has good ideas, and to see them with the same importance as the assignment. Taking notes on one's art and carrying away ideas from it are, after all, the most important reasons for making art.

- *General thoughts to build confidence.* I often give "licenses" and "guarantees" to experiment. With tongue in cheek, I grant licenses such as "The Lifetime License to Experiment in Art." Students who find their own ideas for a lesson, those who find their own way of approaching a work, and those who are not concerned about guessing what the teacher wants from them are entitled to such a license at the end of class.

- *Guaranteeing that "mistakes" cannot be made.* With this license comes my special guarantee, that a student cannot make a mistake in my class. I recognize that throughout the art lesson, problems occur, and sometimes they are so great that there is the temptation to throw out the work. Anyone who is willing to push beyond the difficulties is "guaranteed" to reach new and more significant stages in the work. The belief, therefore, that artworks can be changed—always altered to make them better—has to exist.
- *Challenging thoughts that can be carried beyond the class.* I tell many stories that illustrate the necessity and courage sometimes needed in looking for art all the time and anywhere. I recently held up an exciting bright-red plastic object that I told the class took me a half hour of embarrassment to buy at the discount store. The object did not have a price on it, and the clerk needed to check the price. She asked me what it was; I announced that I did not know. She, and many others in the line, were wondering why this person was buying this item without knowing what it was. Since I thought it would be a great painting tool, I did not give up. The next question was, "What is it used for?," as she attempted to find out what department it was listed under. With more embarrassment, I had to answer that I did not know. When I told her I did not remember what aisle it came from, it did not help matters. As artists, we tend to pick up anything, regardless of its intended use. We find things anywhere. We don't even have to know the purpose of their original design or be trained to use them, if we can freely project onto them our own interests and ideas. One of our most important tasks as artists is to search everywhere, notice everything, and bring it to share in class.

If a teacher prepares a final statement regularly, then students can look forward to it. The teacher's final statement might consist of:

- an informal statement of what the teacher has learned, his or her findings and summary of the lesson;
- a discussion of innovations, new discoveries, unusual solutions suggested in class works;
- a review of students' handling of the art process; attitudes, feelings, and work habits exhibited during the lesson;
- a comparison of the lesson's introduction with the variety and complexity of students' ideas as exhibited in the responses;

- a discussion of the expansion of art ideas and experiences beyond the art room into new investigations and future artworks;
- an expansion of the lesson's ideas to the works of other artists, designers, and media.

For students such statements are often the most meaningful aspect of the lesson; the teacher uses them to communicate feelings, thoughts, and advice that can be lost in the daily round of lessons and class routines. These are certainly lost if the end of the lesson consists of nothing but instructions for cleanup, and class announcements. Students should leave class with a continued interest in their work, a respect for their creative abilities, and an enhanced appreciation of art. The teacher's final statement can promote such attitudes. A final discussion with students at the end of a lesson allows them to express their thoughts and feelings about what they have created; it also allows them to return to the everyday world from the level of heightened thought and perception that characterizes creativity.

EVALUATING THE LESSON AS A WORK OF ART

Evaluating the lesson is an essential follow-through for teachers, an integral part of lesson planning. Once the lesson has been presented, we must find out how well it succeeded, so that we can build from this experience in planning future lessons.

Students have an enormous impact on the meaning of a lesson and on planning, for it is their response to the lesson that determines its outcome. Many aspects of the plan will change during its presentation, and it is important to note these changes. Although the outcome may be very different from what was initially planned, the plan and the outcome together summarize the lesson's meaning. Teachers learn from students just as students learn from teachers, and we can accept lesson ideas as valid only after testing them repeatedly in class.

Teachers can consider the meaning of a lesson by making notes, by writing about what happened in class, and by discussing the class with students. Evaluations should focus on the lesson's visual and creative merits: Was the lesson inventive? Did it attempt to show unusual and interesting visual ideas in its conception and presentation? Was the lesson beautiful? Did it contain beautiful things for the students to see? Did it communicate its intentions with beautiful objects? Did the lesson demonstrate elements of the creative process, including play, search, and reference to art or artists? Did the lesson elicit interest, curiosity, a desire to respond creatively? A visual lesson, well planned, goes beyond the lesson's content: It communicates the nature of the creative process and expresses the beauty of the subject.

By continually learning, as we experiment with new teaching ideas, we avoid becoming trapped in a repetitive routine. The outcome of each lesson is a surprise, and the opportunities for trying new ideas (or devising new performances for ideas that we have used before) are endless. The ideas we are working with can never bore us, because they are the ones that we ourselves most enjoy working with, and we are always moving on to new ones.

When the lessons we teach are our own individual creations from start to finish, we know that we are functioning at our full creative potential; we know that at the center of our work, both as artists and teachers, is the creation of works of art. This fulfills the vision we had of our profession as young artists planning to be teachers. The job would be easier with better funding and greater public respect for art, but the truly essential requirement for such art teaching is the determination of art teachers to bring art—as artists know it—into the classroom. If we have that determination, our creative skills will do the rest.

FOUR SAMPLE LESSONS

The style of writing a lesson or drawing one is individual and must be close to the style of visualizing it. In planning, I find it most effective to freely write and sketch lesson ideas in a narrative, as the following examples show, rather than the usual checklist forms. My lessons have the following common elements:

1. A description of how I visualize the lesson's setting—in other words, what is to be seen, heard, or felt in the room. This includes the design for use of space, display of tools and materials, and arrangement of surfaces.
2. The preparation experiences that students are asked to participate in, sometimes a day or even a week ahead of the lesson.
3. Introductory play, including both teacher performances to introduce and draw students into the lesson and student play to explore the lesson's possibilities and develop ideas for it.
4. A show-and-tell session using beautiful objects, collections, or artworks related to the lesson to suggest possibilities and give a broad view of the subject.

5. An introductory statement, which can be the recollection of a fantasy, a story, a skit, or a poem, to verbally inspire performance.
6. Ideas for changing and altering the lesson at various points, such as play with the lesson's timing or moving participants from one activity or one surface to another.
7. Student and teacher experiences that are used to end the lesson, including the teacher's final statements and students' explorations to help them see beyond the lesson and work to extend it.

Although the lesson examples will include most of these items, they will not always be in the same order, and some may be used more than once in a lesson. All of the following lessons are based on children's play.

Lesson 1: Block Play
Structuring the Three-dimensional Environment,
as Inspiration for Structuring Two-dimensional Surfaces

The sign on the door states "Enter with Care." The students are envisioned as entering carefully and walking among large stacks of wooden alphabet blocks. Other blocks in their containers are placed on different pieces of furniture as future bases to build from—some blocks are placed on chairs, others on the art-room shelf, others are on a high stack of books, and still others under the table. These blocks are from my special collection of antique and new block-related toys, ranging from old Legos to Bristle Blocks, Locblocks, Slinky Shapes, Shape Builders, Magna Sticks, and Tinker Toys. I have also prepared a stack of blocks with soft pencils taped to them.

A week before, students were asked to find their own modular shapes, which could not be store-bought blocks but objects that could be similarly assembled. Students were asked to note possibilities in their idea books and to bring in samples of some of their finds such as clothespins, hair curlers, marshmallows on toothpicks, and ping-pong balls with Velcro, which were displayed in the classroom during the week.

As the students enter the room, the teacher is balancing a long Lego construction between two tables. With an ample supply of space and extra Legos around, students join in to help form the missing links in the ongoing construction. As students find additional block sets around the room, many of which they have not used before, they are eager to try them.

Toward the end of the construction phase, drawing tools and surfaces are discussed as the teacher displays a collection of unusual stencils used by engineers, chemists, architects, and designers. Also, a collection of rulers and graph papers used in these professions is unwrapped, and so is a special box labeled the "Block Box." Inside, students find an outstanding variety of labels, stickers, and stamps (which are in the shape of blocks), and then begin to draw.

The teacher's conversation throughout the lesson consists of challenges to block play: Who can create the longest, most intricate, most unusual stacks, and so forth. The words are designed to encourage students to look at their constructions in terms of unusual events, such as "make believe you are flying over your blocks as you look at them," "make believe a storm or earthquake hit your blocks," "draw as if the blocks were viewed by ants." The teacher also discusses different possibilities of noting a three-dimensional object through tracing its outlines, drawing its shadows, wrapping its forms, photocopying its shapes, or videotaping its fall.

Concluding discussions are envisioned as growing out of my description of babysitting for Aaron, a neighbor's child. Even though toys were in abundance in Aaron's environment, at all stages of his life he preferred construction with three-dimensional forms. As a baby, he liked pulling out objects from the closet and placing one inside another, and now he favors putting chairs together and covering them with blankets, or developing what he calls "setups," by structuring all the books in the playroom as homes and castles for play objects. I plan to conclude with thoughts on the education of an architect who is able to continue as an adult to play and structure with blocks in designing the environment.

Lesson 2: Playing Doctor
The Environment as a Resource for Tools, Materials, and Art Processes

A collection of old toy doctor's kits is displayed in the showcase. Drawing tools are prepared in a collection of old lunchboxes, which, for this experience, are labeled "Dr.'s Bags." The teacher is dressed in operating-room clothes, with mask, hat, and disposable paper shoes.

Materials are set up in several areas of the room. There is a table covered with a roll of white paper, labeled "Operating Table." In another corner, a sheet of plastic hanging from the ceiling is labeled "X-ray." Another table has a roll of adding-machine paper taped to its side, coming out of a box labeled "EKG." Another table has white plastic plumbing parts, labeled "Transplants." On another table, labeled "Blood Bank," are plastic syringes filled with red paint. Another table is covered with cardboard boxes with white sheets of paper labeled "Computer Scanning." As students enter, each receives a name tag ("Dr. _____" [name of student]) and is taken on a tour of the hospital.

The teacher describes a recent hospital experience in assisting his wife in the delivery of their new baby and tells about the various collections and ideas he found in the hospital visit. During the discussion, students try on and experience objects found in a container labeled "Sterile: For Medical Staff Only"—gloves, aprons, and other disposable items, including a strip of EKG tape—which are discussed in terms of art supplies and art surfaces to work on. The teacher demonstrates a drawing series he made on the inside of discarded hospital folders. Students join in the discussion, relating their own experiences with doctors and some of the possibilities of adapting their findings to artworks. We imagine art made with bandages, a make-believe pharmacy dispensing strange "sculptural" pills, or inflatable organ sculptures. The teacher praises all unusual ideas, even if they cannot be made from the available supplies, and encourages students to realize that the ideas are artworks in themselves and can be placed in their idea books.

During the art session, students rotate from one "hospital station" to another, exploring each one and figuring out such activities as doing a workup for a patient or drawing a chart of the patient's health. Some children create imaginative drawings as they lie on a sheet of paper and trace their bodies and try to envision what is inside.

Lesson 3: Dressing Up Play
Discovery of the Many Selves
as Portrait Subjects and as Personalities for Making Art

A corner of the room is set up as a dressing room, with a collection of mirrors, including truck mirrors, makeup mirrors, mirror tiles. Each is covered with plastic Saran Wrap so students can look at themselves and draw right on the mirror. Several suitcases are placed in full view, with labels—"Hats," "Disguises," "Noses," "Scarves," "Masks," and "Makeup."

As students enter, the classroom is dark. They are escorted to their seats with flashlights by other students. The teacher is visible, trying on a collection of funny glasses. As suitcases are opened to reveal the teacher's collection of other items to wear to dress up, students are told of a need to go "underground" and develop a new identity. The teacher begins a strange, scary story, which the students add to and complete in detailing their new identities. Each character will be fully revealed in the new outfit and personal identification card that the wearer will have. The teacher's discussion centers around art as a transformation: how artists can change anything, alter what they see and experience, and even create things that have not existed before. During the dress-up session, students develop many possibilities for recording these new looks in drawings. Some decide to make Garbage Pail Kids cards of themselves. Others draw themselves, and make believe they are putting on makeup in adding color to their picture. Other students begin to feel their new parts and approach their drawings as if the character were doing the drawing.

At an art-party fashion show at the end, students display themselves and wear their artwork made from the disguise or by the disguised person.

Lesson 4: Playing Store
Discovering Color Inspirations, Choices,
and Arrangements Found in Everyday Experiences

In playing out an art-store idea, the room is set up as a diner. Some of the tables have paper tablecloths and place mats. One table becomes an ice cream shop, while the art cart is covered and labeled "Portable Pastry Tray." Another table is marked "Reserved for Restaurant Guests"; a long paper on a wall becomes a freezer, and the teacher's desk becomes a stove. As students enter, the teacher is wearing a chef's hat and is surrounded by old flea-market mixers, pots and pans, and baking tools such as spatulas, as he or she mixes colors placed on a circular piece of cardboard inside a pizza box.

The teacher discusses making and displaying food as an art form, starting with the table setting, the preparation of food, the decoration of items as a design in shape, pattern, and color. The teacher pulls out his or her own collection of food-related items from behind the make-believe freezer, such as menus from restaurants, paintings of pizzas on frisbees, and "greeting cards" designed as slices of bread on which one can place sandwich items such as cold cuts, pickles, or onions. There is an ice cream cart, a box of beautiful chocolates, and unusual lollipops in different colors and sizes. The teacher talks about the many young children she or he has observed and worked with who have served fantastic make-believe meals, and shows the students a book of sculptor Claes Oldenburg's store, with its make-believe food displays.

Mixing yogurt at lunchtime is suggested as a color-mixing experiment. Using an assortment of hats representing different fast-food stores, bakeries, pizza shops, and candy stores, all students are licensed to go into a business and to create competitively food items of beauty to be seen, felt, smelled, and even eaten!

5

Evaluation and Recognition
of Student Performance

Most school review is guided by experts or teacher opinions and reflects the teacher's standards. My principle review strategy has been for students to learn about their own work as much as possible and to rely heavily on their own evaluation. Students learn to look for signs of progress and change within their own works by comparing new works in a series or new works with old art and with the work of other artists they may admire. Stress is placed not only on evaluating the artwork but on examining one's goals and ideas as recorded in student idea books. Students are asked to review the "state of their art" by utilizing examples of their artworks and those artworks that are ideas not yet realized.

Using a single artwork, or the end product of the art-making process, as the basis for evaluating students' work can be deceptive for several reasons. An end product does not reflect the various stages in which the work was made—the critical planning stage or the experiments that preceded the actual making. Evaluation must also take into account the changes and adjustments that were made, and the new learning that occurred, during the making of the work. As noted earlier, students' ability to learn while they are working, to incorporate new ideas, and to change and improve the work while they are making it are all important indications of competency. We therefore need to find ways of recording such changes and innovations during the art-making process. The traditional assumption that the finished artwork must "match" the description given in the original plan for the work is mistaken, since it leaves no room for creative change during the art making and penalizes, rather than rewarding, independent decision making. Sometimes the ideas that have been explored during the art process leave no trace in the final product. A single work may present a range of exploration, demonstrating several different competencies.

The complexity of the art process makes the final product an inaccurate demonstration of all of the student's abilities.

Visual learning appears to have its own sequence, which may be different from verbal demonstrations of learning. A single work cannot fully represent all of the different long-range plans and ongoing projects that the artist has in mind. Students who speak of ideas or display abilities that seem to indicate that they have mastered a certain set objective may produce an artwork that demonstrates no trace of it. Artists previsualize solutions several phases in advance, and the artist's present work may not yet have entered the stage that he or she is projecting for the future. What students say they have learned from a work may be different from what others perceive, since students may be looking backward or forward, thinking in terms of their long-range plans. We need forms of evaluation that permit us to see more of the process that students go through in making their works and to trace their developing interests and adaptive strategies.

It clearly is helpful to sample the progress during the initial planning stages and during the art making. Discussions with students during both of these stages will help. Student records in sketches or drawings, photographs, videotapes, or films provide a permanent record of the works' progress. Teachers can also make sketches and notes to aid our memories later.

If we have succeeded in encouraging students to develop a sequence of works, the sequence will reveal more than a single work could about the learning that has occurred. We must be sure to store each student's works carefully during the term so that the entire series is available for review when the term ends.

EVALUATING ONE'S OWN WORK

At the conclusion of an art lesson, I often ask students to put up their artworks on the display boards around the room. As the works begin to fill the space, I review them with excitement and pride. My being openly joyful at seeing beautiful works around me often leads to conversations with the students, many of whom do not see, feel, or share my joy or understand my reasons for celebration. One group of students is satisfied not because they appreciate their own accomplishments but because they have made the teacher happy, which they feel will lead to a good grade. Others have created innovative and beautiful works but have little comprehension of their merit or beauty and hence would never show or display these works in their homes. Then

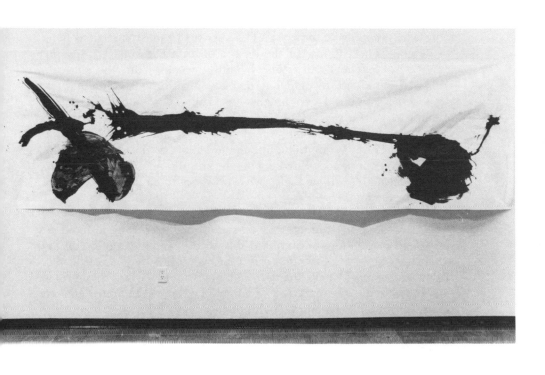

*Scroll paintings: Visualizations from the study
of children's early attempts at alphabet formation.*

there is always that small but vocal group of students who openly hate their works and don't see what I could possibly admire in them.

After these exchanges with my students, I inwardly adjust my celebrations and begin reexamining a lesson that indeed produced beautiful art but failed to teach students how to comprehend their own work and accomplishments. How can students be taught to see and feel in their own art a sense of beauty and invention and begin to understand its possibilities? How can students get to know their own artworks better? What concepts of art are students taking away with them when they leave the class? The answers to these questions have far-ranging implications for the design of an art lesson. True, some creative art teachers can "pull" beautiful works from the students without the students' recognizing their accomplishments; but completing teacher-suggested assignments according to teacher-prescribed outlines to gain a teacher's approval does not tell a student why a project was done. A teacher's simple judgment that a work is of high quality does not say anything about the value for the student of the work or the experience of making it. The aim should always be to help students learn to evaluate their own works, not to have others provide the final assessment.

Too often, students are taught *what* to see, not *how* to see. One can always spot art students in a museum; they are filling in handout sheets and responding to questions designed to focus attention on the artworks. They may provide correct answers, but they can still miss seeing and experiencing the art. Telling students what to see in a museum—or in their own work—can only be done in the most general terms, or students' responses will not be creative and personal; they will be limited by what they feel they are "supposed to see." Really seeing an artwork is not a matter of responding to questions raised by someone else but of posing relevant questions oneself.

Students who understand the works they have created are able to set goals for themselves and, by examining each new work at various stages of completion, guide their artworks during the process of creation. Once a work is completed, they are able to describe it, assess it, and compare it with previous efforts; they can read in it clues to the utilization of the experiences it has provided. They go beyond the story or subject of their works to grasp their aesthetic qualities: lines, spaces, surfaces, forms, and other features. They understand how the tools and materials used have worked for them, they proceed from this examination of their works to self-examination, for each new work gives them a surer sense of their capabilities and interests. They have learned about themselves as artists from having gone through the process of producing the work. Students therefore need to recognize links between one work and the next, to recognize ideas that are worth exploring in future endeavors. The more we know our work, the better we are able to guide ourselves from one work to the next. Students who really know their artworks and who through their works have examined the process and experience of making art are able to devise both short- and long-term goals.

For the artist, the most important aspect of an artwork is the promise it holds for future works, both in the insight that is gained through its execution and in the ideas it reveals concretely. If we look carefully, we see that each work is an important preparation for the next one. A final test of students' comprehension of their works is the ability to evaluate the work of other artists. In fact, students who are able to evaluate their own works are generally more open to the ideas of others, even those that are unusual or nontraditional. If they can learn from the works of others, then they can learn from their own. Such learning becomes a lifelong task and art a lifelong teacher.

Verbal Evaluation

Frequently, I walk around schools visiting classes with well-meaning administrators. When we come into an art room, they often ask students who appear to be deeply involved in art that they are doing. The students invariably reply, "I don't know." Of course these students are working with many ideas and often know exactly what they are doing, but they find it difficult to verbalize what they know, since there are few opportunities in art classes to talk about artworks. Such a response from people who are deeply involved in visual thinking and planning does not reflect well on an art program. The aim of art instruction is not just planning art and understanding it, but articulating this understanding. If a lesson is planned well, not only can the teacher understand and communicate its intentions, but the students can also communicate clearly to others what they are doing. Young artists can guide their works better and will be more conscious of their internal plans and choices when they are able to talk about their work. The verbalization of ideas is important in the final evaluation of a work. Students need to develop a descriptive language of art so that they can comfortably discuss their works; otherwise, they will rely too heavily on the language of the teacher and will never come to understand their art.

All artists are engaged in a continuous dialogue with each work. This dialogue can be clarified by the artist's discussing the work with different people. By presenting their ideas to others—by talking or preparing real or imaginary brochures, news releases, slide shows, or lectures—students learn about their own works. They focus on what is in the work as much as the audience does. They learn about the philosophy or conviction that went into shaping the work and can therefore better direct future works. Words are vehicles of long-term visions.

If students need to discuss their works, then they need an audience. In art class the student's audience is the teacher and the other students. The art teacher needs to be an audience to the students' dreams and ideas, both to help them understand what they have accomplished and to help new works come to fruition. I recently expressed delight with a beautiful painting a student had made, but she felt only disgust and anger with the painting. "I struggled with this painting for days, but it doesn't reflect the ideas I wanted to express." She went on to tell me in detail what she really wanted to paint. It was my job, as the teacher, not to offer an opinion based on my experience and expectations but to be a supportive listener. By doing so, I helped the student see her ideas more clearly and feel greater confidence in developing them.

Art teachers can help students not just by listening but also by asking imaginative questions. Such questioning encourages students to explore their works playfully and creatively: They can take stock of what they have accomplished in a particular work or look beyond it by considering how its ideas could be extended. The teacher's questions can focus on the structure of a work or on its ideas and intentions. Questioning may include the use of playful ideas—for example, asking students to make believe they are flying over their own work or picking a basketful of colors from it. Even questions that sound ridiculous can be useful in creating a new mood, a new frame of reference for evaluating the work. For example, students can be asked to make believe that they have a magic pair of scissors that lets them cut out special parts of an artwork, revealing specific qualities, or magic glasses that pick up only certain details or colors in a work, or the means of making an artwork talk and "describe" itself in terms of certain criteria. If the colors of one's work were made of ice and melted, what would the result look like? If the shapes in a work were made of clay, how could they be molded and stuck together? If you had to advertise the unique qualities of your work in a flyer or announcement, what would the headlines say? Through such imaginary situations, students can change the work, draw information from it, or develop ideas on what they now see in it.

Through skillful questioning, a teacher can promote students' understanding of their works and encourage them to continue to explore interesting ideas. Although a teacher's discussing or questioning a student's work can be fruitful, such activities must be handled with care. Simply telling a student what the teacher likes or dislikes about a work does not allow the student to develop self-confidence and understanding. Group criticism, after a student presents his or her work for discussion, can be uncomfortable, embarrassing, and often counterproductive. Teachers can prevent this situation by allowing time for discussion, especially at the end of class. Although students deserve privacy and choice, and consequently should not be asked to present their works until they feel ready to do so, eventually they will have to present their works. Furthermore, the judgments of others play an important role in students' perception of their works. Discussion not only helps students deal with their own reactions; it also helps them deal with the reactions of others. Discussion can allay disappointment and help students see what is valuable about a work. Teachers can point out that our immediate reactions do not always accurately reflect the quality of the finished work. It is reassuring to be told that many great artworks were first judged to be great by their creators or by the art audience long after they were created.

Through discussion students realize that each viewer brings something different to a work and that consequently different viewers respond differently to the same work. Each work will have its supporters and its critics. Furthermore, viewers may not be aware of the problems or goals of the artist, and this too can color their perception of a work. Discussion allows young artists to clarify their intentions and also helps them see reasons for audience response to their work. Although students should learn to be open to audience response, they should also learn to stand up for their ideas. It is important that students believe in their creative abilities and in what they have to offer. Students can be reminded that great art ideas usually have limited audiences and that the more experimental, thoughtful, and personal art becomes, the less an audience may appreciate it.

Through observing the teacher's thoughtful and supportive responses, students can learn how to be a good audience. They learn how to listen to one another and how to learn from one another. Instead of viewing others' works impatiently and making quick judgments based on unconsidered beliefs, students learn to remain open to new ideas and new approaches. One of the best ways for students to learn to evaluate art is to discuss their work with each other in class. Learning to be a good audience for art and learning how to deal with audience reaction to one's own art is part of learning to be an artist. Students may want to talk about the experience of creation and show others what they have created. Through presenting their works to others, they learn by listening to themselves, and often, through the discussion and presentation, something new is revealed.

Visual Evaluation

Student-made videos are an excellent means of sharing ideas and reflecting on the artist's discoveries. One student, for example, demonstrated her discovery of soft, clear plastic as a drawing surface by demonstrating how the soft plastic could be draped on a face, could cling to a window or television screen, or be laid over a mirror or photograph and used to trace the images in them. In her presentation she explained how, through these processes, she had arrived at a multilayered finished drawing. Another student made a video demonstrating his new technique called "twin" drawing. Taping pairs of crayons to each finger, the student had composed a "piano-concert" drawing, using parallel lines. One of my favorite videos was by a student who described some of his difficulties in creating art and how the resulting paintings were planned to cope with his problems. The student said he preferred to work on patterned papers, since they already had some image on them, and therefore, he did not have to face the more frightening empty white sheet. He explained that he used large, simple forms, such as a bow or a ball, since they did not involve the distractions of drawing and could be painted immediately with pure color, which was also less frightening. The ability of this elementary-school student to retrace clearly his art process, and his response to solving problems related to the work, were a result of preparing a video communication.

Inter-artist Communications

Since artists direct their own work, they must also be able to evaluate it, learning from past successes and failures and comparing it to the work of other artists, both past and present. Every artist is also an art critic and an art historian, keenly interested in learning from other artists and in understanding art concepts. Artists learn a great deal by sharing art ideas with other artists, and most of us feel that belonging to a circle of artist friends is an important part of our lives. Artists know that a work of art must not only satisfy the artist but must communicate the artist's vision to others, for art is a form of communication.

Through the mail, I keep in touch with artist friends, exchanging images by way of "post-card" artworks, including special greeting cards, show announcements, and pictures we draw for each other. We write descriptions of our work and discuss our problems. We mail pages from our sketchbooks and we describe our present works and our hopes for future ideas; occasionally, we mail artworks to each other, on loan.

Over the phone, we listen to long descriptions of images of each others' works and observations. Simply listening to them while we visualize over the phone helps us to clarify our own images and recognize our dreams. We share leads to a new find or the problems of getting on with a work. Most importantly, we reassure each other that we are still working, that our work is still worthwhile, and that we exist for one another as a caring audience. Communication between colleagues can be a valuable model for students in evaluating and learning about their own art.

Evaluation through Drama

Role playing, in the form of skits and plays, can be used to get students to focus on their art ideas and on the details, innovations, and experiences involved in their creation. Artists talk about their work and talk to their work. Students can:

- interview an artwork by holding a microphone up to its surface and "listening" to the work's response.
- prepare make-believe sound tracks or narrations to a film that reflects on their art selections.
- wear selected artwork and narrate the fashion show to include commentaries on its innovations.
- auction their most famous pieces. The auctioneer's voice describes the works' contributions to the art world.
- create poems in homage to an artwork, paying special attention to visual qualities and innovations.
- play the roles of gallery owners as they compose rejection and acceptance letters to famous artists.

Some of the most memorable comments of well-known artists can be read in their letters to friends and dealers. Students can talk about their most intimate ideas and feelings about artworks in a similar format. Learning to think of themselves as artists, they will have attained a new self-confidence, and indeed a new identity, having discovered the artist within themselves.

Discussions can help students deal with disappointment in their artwork or with their classmates' criticisms. While the adult artist has the luxury of withholding works from audiences until he or she decides they are ready for viewing, young artists have difficulty shielding their works from immediate public response. In class, they are always surrounded by an audience, and they often receive comments on a work before they have had a chance to assess it themselves and to consider how they might defend it. As they work, they are always aware of what their classmates consider successful, ridiculous, or disappointing. Such awareness can stifle new ideas, and criticism from peers, especially when offered prematurely, can bruise young egos.

USING ART TO EVALUATE ART

Students can be helped to learn to evaluate their own art by making new works in response to their finished works. They can imitate the original artwork; vary the medium, movement, scale, materials, or even the techniques used to produce the work; or simply examine the art through drawings or sculptures used in the creation of the work or created from it. Imitating the art—that is, restating or copying it—helps the artist to explore feelings and ideas that occurred at various stages of the work and to recapture the inspiration. Giving the work a new format—translating it, so to speak—also provides an interesting perspective. When the color, scale, or medium is changed, the work is changed, allowing us to make comparisons with the original and with the experience of working with the original. Each new work made in response to the original is an interpretation of it, a reaction to it that the artist can learn from and incorporate into the new work; he or she rethinks the work in its new format. For the inexperienced artist, it is often easier to explore and clarify a work using art processes than to comment on it verbally.

The new format chosen depends on what one is looking for. Rubbings, for example, may be useful in exploring the feeling of the surfaces of a piece of architecture. Using the structural possibilities of sculpting, we can study two-dimensional art by translating it into three-dimensional form and examining the outline, texture, and shape. To further study the lines of a painting, we can bend linear material such as strings or wires to approximate the feeling, movement, and line qualities of the original or cut, fold, or tear tapes to approximate the lines. We can add color to reproductions of the student's artwork to find new possibilities regarding color and shape. Photocopies can provide innumerable positive and negative images that can be freely cut, torn, and marked over. Drawing directly from an artwork gives us the opportunity to study it intently so that details can be observed and remembered. Even simple devices such as tracing paper or carbon paper allow the quick diagramming of an artwork. Such diagramming is useful, for it gives us easy access to the work. We can obtain numerous copies without having to draw them, a difficult and sometimes tedious task. We can therefore move more quickly from the diagramming to a study of the art itself.

Techniques for Evaluating One's Own Art

Let us now take a more detailed look at some techniques that can be used for learning to evaluate one's art. I have found these to be effective with children from kindergarten to twelfth grade.

Mapping and Diagramming. Drawings can be used to record and illustrate ideas found in a student's art. The drawings are actually quick sketches that summarize the student's observations and so are different from standard drawings. Practice is needed to develop the speed and the requisite freedom to execute such sketches. Mappings, or diagrams, of a work can be executed on top of duplicates such as slide projections, photocopies, or tracings. The result is a visual aid to the investigation of the work, filled with personal marks that may be meaningful only to the artist. Thus, the student comes to understand his or her own work.

Tracings. Diagrams of two-dimensional artworks made by placing tracing paper directly on top of a work can reveal a great deal to the young artist. Each transparent layer can be used to explore different aspects of the work, such as form or color placement; the transparent layers reveal how different elements relate to each other and to the edge of the work. Patterns, textures, and shapes are clarified when individual tracings are made of each detail, or the artist can simply gain a feeling for the work by going over the tracings. Paintings, drawings, and prints are frequently created in layers, so by using overlays the artist can study each layer—and hence each idea—individually. The artist can also place one layer on top of another to see how the work has evolved.

Coverings.   Students can wrap or cover three-dimensional works to discover their form. The act of covering simplifies the form by adding a sort of skin; we focus not on the function or subject of the work but on its shapes and edges. When foil, plastic, tracing paper, and cloth are used as coverings, details are outlined and edges defined. Coverings may be loose or tightly wrapped to reveal in detail what is underneath. Each side of a three-dimensional form can be traced to record its shape, and when material like foil is used, the covering, once removed, can serve as a quick and simple mold. Even the use of light—with variance in distance, direction, and level—can reveal a form, sharpening our understanding of it.

Cutting Apart and Placing Together.   Students can learn about the composition of a work by cutting apart a reproduction of it. When students evaluate a work, they take it apart visually; they can learn how to evaluate by actually taking the work apart with scissors. Two-dimensional artworks all have a frame. Cutting a work apart can help students learn about its forms and lines and how they combine to make a whole within that frame. Duplicates of each work can be cut up differently, for different purposes, to gain a strong sense of how the artwork has been constructed. Works can be taken apart and put back together like a puzzle. Students can even display parts of a work that has been cut up. Color areas or shapes cut from a work become guides to understanding. Treating the cut-up work like a puzzle in reverse, students can study the whole image and the relationship of its parts to the whole.

Estimating.   All works consist of lines and shapes that can be estimated—imitated in another medium—to learn more about them. By tracing the lines of a drawing with wire placed on top of it, or ripping and cutting out of paper some of the shapes found in the work, students come to understand the original. Clay can be used to estimate a work's form and the result placed next to the original for comparison. If students make clay versions of completed sculptures, they have a chance to make adjustments.

Estimating yields a rich array of new works that make immediately accessible to the students all the elements that make up the original. These works help the student focus on edges, directions, the size of shapes, the quality of lines, connections and divisions, color areas, and patterns. Not only do they show us what we see; they show us what we missed when making the original. Estimating allows an active participation in a work that clarifies it for its maker.

Framing. Whatever we look at is given a frame by our vision. Whatever we create also has its own frame, which needs to be identified and studied. Reframing a work can teach students about the framing process. Paper or cardboard frames of different sizes and shapes can be placed around a work to reveal the relationship of the edge to the work itself. With pencil or tape, students can create new borders that reveal the structure of the work: the divisions, relationships, and patterns formed by its edge. A camera lens enables them to study the work in segments, so that they can focus on details or areas they may like or may want to change. Since they are not tied tightly to the original edge, they can rethink the work's composition. Thus, framing exercises not only make students more aware of the frame and its effect on the relationships set up in the work, but they also loosen, and thereby revitalize, students' perceptions of the artwork.

Enlarging and Reducing. Changing the scale of a work makes its creator more keenly aware of the work itself. Like any alteration of a work, enlargement or reduction calls for careful observation of the original, which allows the young artist to understand it better. The entire work or only sections or details can be enlarged, reduced, or serialized. Individual enlargements of a section or detail fit together to provide a review of the whole piece. Students can engage in numerous enlargement and reduction experiments, all of which can assist them in reevaluating their own works in detail. Seeing work in a different scale not only offers a new view of it but suggests exciting possibilities beyond the original.

Simplification and Elaboration. Simplifying a work is something an artist does continuously while making it. Students can learn about their works by adopting this approach, pruning areas or details that may not work or are not related to a student's central concerns. Simplifying can be accomplished visually or by cutting out, erasing, painting over, covering up, or otherwise refining segments of a work or its reproductions. Teachers can have students cover up certain details as they trace over the original or ask them to describe a complex work in three lines or shapes to help them clarify its principal ideas. Or students can be asked to outline the work, essentially reducing it to its main forms. By simplifying, students learn to state the original more precisely. One can also learn about the original by expanding a work, elaborating it, creating more complex versions. By recognizing how they have changed the original, students learn to understand their work.

GETTING A NEW PERSPECTIVE

There are other ways of getting a fresh perspective on a work besides making other artworks. Simply placing the work in a new position can give one a different view of it. Placing a sculpture in a new setting gives the sculpture a new life. Works can be viewed from different angles by turning them sideways or upside down. These playful turnings change the relationship of the framing edge and baseline, suggesting new compositional possibilities. Works can be viewed on the floor, on a wall or table, across the room, or close up at different eye levels. They can even be taken outdoors, where a new environment and different lighting will reveal new space and object relationships. A work can be examined on its own or displayed in a selected arrangement with other works for a comparative viewing. Covering different parts of a work with paper or our hands isolates areas, letting us focus on selected details and breaking up relationships that may be too firmly set in our minds. Looking at a work in these different ways alters the familiar perceptions we have of it and suggests to us new possibilities.

Projections of a work using a slide projector provide another format through which an artwork can be examined. The artwork is reproduced in a variety of scales, making it readily accessible to redrawing and tracing exercises. Students can draw on, scratch, carve, or punch holes in the slides to facilitate examination of the projections. They can also work on the projected image, learning how the impact of the work changes as its size and scale change and gathering information from diagrams done on the screen. Projections allow students to choose from many versions of a work and to examine its details individually or together by creating composites of slide images. All sorts of creative alterations of the projected image are possible: It can be viewed upside down or out of focus, or projected over forms, colors, and textures. Through playful projection, students can learn to see their works differently and discover new possibilities within them.

Video screens provide a different learning experience. Projections on a video screen are continuous, stopped only by the viewer's needs. Changes in specific details are heightened through sequential viewing, which provides a journey over and through the work. Aerial views of a work's surface, closeups, freeze-frames, and views from all possible angles are available. The moving images on the screen duplicate the eye's searching through a work. Through video screens, students become their own audience.

Photographers look through their fingers to frame the subject of a photograph; painters frequently use a thumb as a tool of measurement. Simple devices familiar to children can be used to create new conditions for viewing artworks. Students often enjoy using binoculars or telescopes to look at their works. Magnifying glasses, plastic mirrors, and magnification sheets allow multiple angles, multiple views, and closeups of areas or details. Car, truck, or makeup mirrors, Mylar, and mirror sheets create reversed images and unusual wide-angled views. All of these devices give students a sense of freedom that enables them to see their works in a new light.

THE ART EXHIBIT
AS A TEACHING TOOL

There is nothing like a show! My own exhibits in Soho (in New York City) over the past twelve years have been invaluable in my artistic development. Although each show required endless preparation, it brought me new understanding of art that I could not have acquired in any other way. Exhibitions require the most thorough knowledge of one's work, gained through the detailed study and careful comparison of one's productions. Because of this experience, I wanted to explore the educational possibilities of exhibits for young artists. With the aid of funding from the University of Kentucky, I have organized three programs in Kentucky to demonstrate the possibilities of learning through thoughtful art exhibits. One is the Gallery Internship Program for young artists to take part in preparations of gallery and museum exhibits by professional artists. The second is a program called Gallery Owners, which allows students within the schools to maintain and operate designated spaces as their own art galleries for mounting a series of exhibits. Finally, I have organized demonstration exhibits in the schools, which are called Kentucky Exhibition Models, in which assistance and support is given to creative art exhibitions.

Most typically in the schools, finished artworks are stored or, sometimes, selected by the teacher for a hallway display. For the artist, however, finished works are extremely important to have around, since they represent clues and become teachers in making decisions about further works. Having works hung informally in the studio or as part of an exhibit helps one to learn from one's product. Through the many active steps of exploring and comparing completed artworks, exhibitions provide opportunities for reflection and decision making by the artist. In preparing an exhibit, the artist views the work not only as its maker but as a potential audience.

School art displays usually tend to be hallway decorations and nothing more. Because they are not prepared by students, they do not provide the kind of learning experiences that can take place before, during, and after the mounting of an exhibit for the student artist and audience. With some help from the teacher, exhibitions can expand from the bulletin boards inside the school or the refrigerator door at home to the larger community, so that student art is communicated to a wider audience.

The Kentucky Exhibition Models (1984–1986) have demonstrated the value of using exhibitions as tools for helping students learn about their art and act independently in deciding on future artworks. In considering art exhibits as art forms, students also change and develop the art made for them. Artworks that are "completed" by being placed in folders are not finished in the artist's mind until they are presented to and studied by an audience. One learns about one's art from the responsive eye of others, from comments and criticism that make art a communication and therefore complete. The private act of making art needs to be balanced by the public event, including the exchanges between artist and audience, as well as the celebrations that provide additional insight. Well-planned and innovative art exhibits, therefore, bring greater excitement, greater confidence, and greater interest to making art in the first place.

Three years ago, I began to organize the Gallery Internship Program in local galleries and museums in Lexington, Kentucky, for students as young as grade 4. The purpose of the internship program is to have students observe how professional exhibits are mounted and apply their observations to school exhibitions. When possible, students visit the artists' studios to witness the monumental preparations for a show. They observe artists gathering quantities of completed works from which to make their selections, seeing how works are placed side by side, in many different positions and comparative sequences. Details are carefully observed and discussed, and changes and developments in the works are reviewed. The artist observes alone as well as with friends and colleagues, making preliminary choices. Works best representing the artists' idea and those that may contribute to the total presentation are selected. These experiences are impossible in school art when works are unrelated, individually made, and stored. In the studio, artists make sketches and notes for display ideas showing how the works are to be located in relationship to the architectural details, the space, and the viewer. Finally, the works are "dressed" as possibilities for framing are considered (or undressed, for simplicity of presentation). The artists also have to prepare publicity statements and brochures and, through the process of writing, they clarify their own perceptions of their art and summaries of their ideas. Works are then brought to the gallery and provide new experiences as they are moved from the place where they were created, taking on a new independence and appearance under different lights and a new setting. This requires the artists to grasp again the nature of their creation. New selections, comparisons, and reviews are made, since a much larger quantity of work is brought to the gallery than will be exhibited. A new set of preliminary viewers, including the gallery staff, discusses the work and gives reactions. Works are placed in many temporary setups, tried at different heights, angles, and spacings. The art is photographed for brochures, and even viewing it through the camera is an invaluable way of studying one's art. Different lighting is tried, and again the artist has to understand what the best view of the work is. The smallest concerns at the opening, such as the colors of the food served, become part of reflecting and understanding one's work as it is prepared to be shared with others.

Each student in my classes owns a gallery. No, these are not special classes for wealthy children. They are simply students responsible for a designated space in the school to develop an ongoing gallery schedule presenting artworks of their own, designed objects they have found, or guest exhibits. These exhibits have taken place in hallways, libraries, and gymnasiums. Each show has an idea and a theme, an opening, and suitable advertisement. For some classes, the galleries are small-scale, designed to house miniature exhibits that are models for full-scale art. These "shows in a box" allow students to dream freely in different materials and scales, creating complicated, large exhibits that cannot be funded or prepared in a school. Students learn about preparing exhibits, and each show is discussed with other gallery owners and with audiences. Works for each exhibit are tested in many different selections and placement possibilities, from traditional to highly unusual.

Through the Gallery Owners' Program, students take over exhibition responsibilities usually held by the teacher. While they are learning about the exhibition process and their own art, students also discover audiences—how to involve, interest, and effectively communicate with a public.

In conferences with gallery owners, different exhibition considerations are reviewed by the teacher. New ways for audiences to view a show are considered, and through this process the gallery owner, who is also the artist, learns new ways to see his or her own work. For example, we have used playful movements to encourage new ways of viewing, a richer variety of observations, and, at the same time, an expanded attention span for the young audiences, who have been asked to see shows while walking backward, spinning around, holding their heads sideways, or skipping on one foot. Although these instructions may not be given at the Museum of Modern Art, considering that this is an audience of children these playful viewings are natural and interesting. My gallery owners also frequently distribute simple props for audiences to use to view the show in more detail. Magnifying glasses, binoculars, mirrors, make-believe television cameras, colored glasses, and even flashlights for looking at shows in the dark help to encourage detailed and playful viewing.

Audiences are also asked to examine artworks by remaking them, or to create summary versions of what they see. Standing in the gallery with sketchpads, clay, or wire in their hands, our audiences redraw, retrace, or even sculpt from the exhibited works. We also use innovative media such as Etch-a-Sketch for redrawings and fingers and bodies in make-believe tracings of works.

As gallery owners, students explore their art through written press releases, brochures, and catalogs, as well as through verbal interviews and conversations with audiences. Gallery owners employ a variety of media in preparing a guided-tour tape recording to accompany a show or taking Polaroid pictures for the press release. While each gallery owner plays his or her role, other students are asked to pose as reviewers, art collectors, and even museum guards, to consider different perspectives.

The artist-as-gallery-owner learns a lot from conversations with different audiences. Each show allows the artist to rework ideas many times in his or her mind. The memories of a whole show fade more slowly than those of single works. Because of gallery owners' involvement with audiences, the memory of even a single unusual or sympathetic comment becomes a powerful force for new ideas, or simply an incentive to keep working. If necessary, artworks can be changed after a show or even during a show.

During the past five years, a variety of unusual exhibits supported by this program were held in the Kentucky public schools. Some of the exhibition ideas developed by gallery owners included:

- Various display formats: Audience-participation formats where students were encouraged to touch, rip, hug, or press artworks. These artworks were specifically created to elicit responses and, in fact, be enhanced by audiences who walked on, sat on, altered, and completed the work by their actions. Another format involved portable exhibits to be worn on sandwich boards, attached to broomsticks, rolled on wheels, or used as floats in a parade. Another format was named "The Hidden Exhibit," and one had to look for the art as a hidden treasure in the ground, inside containers, and even in a wall. Multiarts exhibits included the viewing of works accompanied by music, reflected on by dance, or explained through poetry. Finally, formats were used in which the show had its own explanation: Artworks were exhibited together with their sources of inspiration. Sometimes the steps or techniques used in making the work became part of the exhibit. For example, a print show included the plates and even the rollers and mixing trays used to make the work.
- Many unusual display ideas for single works were arrived at through student experiments. We displayed works upside down in an "upside down" show. For another show, we used only the architectural corners of the building, while in another exhibit, we used the works' reflections in mirrors, and the shadows formed through unusual lighting of objects.
- Unusual display places were explored, and shows were created inside an old filing cabinet; under a tent, an umbrella, and a parachute; and inside china cups.
- Among the many show themes was one that highlighted processes, that is, a show with computer art, art made with toys, and so forth. Material themes were also used, including an exhibit of art on bedsheets, tablecloths, and floor tiles.
- We discussed and explored exhibition possibilities involving unusual artistic ideas or actions in preparing the show. We held an exhibit in which all the art was made during the exhibit, while another exhibit contained not works but the student-artists' guided explanations of what the show would have been like had it been placed in the gallery.
- A series of specially funded exhibits included the student-artist exhibiting alongside invited guests. We had shows with the artist and his teachers, siblings, parents, and neighbors. The exhibits with

adults, especially with the teacher, helped lend these exhibits greater interest and legitimacy.

Each exhibit is a celebration, a recognition of achievements by the artist and others viewing it. It is also an opportunity to dress up (oneself and the artwork) and present the work in its best light, best pose, and best location. It is a chance to take a private act and introduce it to the public. Exhibits require conceptualization of one's art in order to create a suitable display environment for it. To celebrate the end of exhibits, we have used many performances, such as students' marching with their work, wearing their work, or having their work come alive and "speak" to audiences. From the choice of costumes to the foods at an opening party, everything can be selected and arranged to reflect on a display. These events can be opportunities to celebrate the art and to make art out of the celebration. For example, we have painted faces to accompany a show of masks; we have made edible, baked art forms for a show of food paintings; and we wore futuristic costumes to an opening of a show of space art. The design of invitations, handouts, lighting, and even souvenir stands provides gallery owners with opportunities to summarize and expand the ideas of the artworks for the public celebration.

Believing in the educational values of student exhibits requires the art teacher to take on the role of exhibition promotor and publicist, looking for places where students can exhibit their works in the community. This means that many community events can be considered as occasions for an art show. Everything from a simple open house at school to the grand opening of a mall, a balloon race, or an antique car show can be investigated as a possibility. When a major store with large display windows is vacant downtown while awaiting a buyer, its windows can become a fine street gallery. When a new building is erected, its wooden barricades are immediately seen by the teacher-promotor as art-display boards. Finally, all social contacts, such as those with parents of students and with one's friends, can be thought of as possible sources of locations for student exhibits. The parent who owns a fish restaurant or gas station suggests interesting themes for nontraditional exhibit areas and subjects: large plastic fishes to swim in the restaurant space, and painted cardboard gas pumps for the gas station site.

During my early teaching days in Staten Island, as I have recounted earlier, I began my first art classes with a drawing trip on the famous Staten Island ferry. Students starting the course with serious doubts about their creative selves gained incredible confidence in being asked to work on the ferry and face curious crowds who assumed they were all artists. It was the combination of being an artist, exhibiting their art (like our gallery owners), and conversing with the audiences on the ferry that made the children begin to feel and talk like artists. Exhibitions have a way of building insights and confidence as no other experiences can. One learns about one's art the moment it is placed in public space and received by audiences.

Each exhibit is an extension of the art, with opportunities to learn about it while the exhibit is being prepared, discussed, and arranged. Students need opportunities to create exhibits as they learn to create artworks. They need to be able to participate in the complete development of a show as they become artists as well as audience and critics. Artists are not certified or licensed, but the feeling that you are an artist is developed through significant experiences, such as showing. Having your own art exhibit is very close to the actor's initial experience on the stage, where performing (or, in this case, exhibiting) simply gets into your blood.

6

The Artist-Teacher

BECOMING AN ARTIST-TEACHER

In the preceding chapters of this book, I have asserted the need for a revolution in art teaching. The emphasis in Chapters 1 through 5 has been on what teachers can do to preserve themselves as artists within the public school system.

All art teachers, at some point during our early development, made the discovery that we were artists, a crucial experience in discovering our identities. All of us hoped to create during our lifetimes work that would express our individual insights; all of us expected to find continual renewal in our work. We knew that art could never be dull or repetitive. We looked forward to passing on our enjoyment of art to our students.

Once we became teachers in the public school system, we worked hard to teach children the fundamentals of art. Knowing how little prestige our subject enjoyed within the schools, we did our best to fit into the school program and teach as we were expected to, although we realized that we were seriously handicapped by the lack of adequate funds, supplies, space, and lesson time. Many of us, because we worked so hard at our teaching, found that we lacked the time and energy to do much work in art. Our lives seemed to revolve around lesson plans, classroom management, and limited student art projects. The excitement of working every day with challenging art ideas and images of visual beauty, which we had enjoyed so greatly in graduate school, was often missing. Nothing in our graduate education or in our situation within the schools helped us to cope with the problem we were experiencing—that of combining art with teaching. Indeed, much of what we were expected to do as teachers seemed so different from our interests and behavior as artists that we reached a discouraging conclusion: If we were to succeed as art teachers, it might have to be at the expense of our personal achievement as artists.

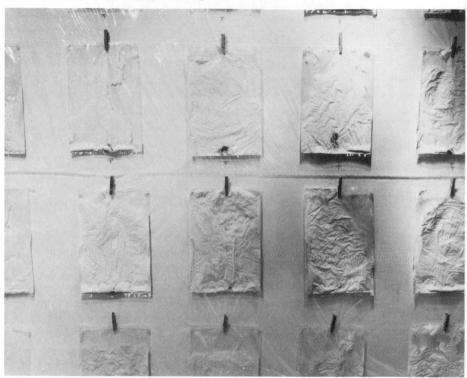

*Compositions with filled paint bags, inspired
by children's paint mixing experiments.*

Some of us blamed ourselves for this situation. We had been naive, we decided, ever to assume that we could fully combine both careers. We should have realized earlier, we told ourselves, that the choice was basically either/or: Either one became an artist, or one became an art teacher. An art teacher would have time to do only a limited amount of creative work; if we spent too much time on our personal work, we would be neglecting our students. As teachers, our students' welfare must be our major concern—and we did care deeply about our students. It had been obvious in graduate school that we were being given a different training from those who planned simply to be artists, and now, in the local school system, no one seemed to feel that the question of whether the art teacher was also a fully functioning professional artist was important. It was quite painful to realize that in becoming teachers we had (without knowing it) basically given up our dream of being artists, but we ourselves were to blame: We just had not understood how things were in teaching.

I once watched this experience of separating the artist from the teacher happen in miniature, within a few days rather than over a period of years, with one of my young graduate students. Karen made the most beautiful series of prints produced in classes in 1970. I remember how she gently inked tree trunks around the college campus for printing, and the sight of the trees being covered with soft white wrappings, held on with plastic strings, as each tree waited to be rubbed. Karen designed an "unwrapping" ceremony that we all attended as part of the presentation. Then, the following week, she showed me some prints she had made with the children in her public school classes. These small, precut Valentine cards, printed with linoleum blocks, were all similar, even in the stock papers used, and bore little resemblance to the excitement in Karen's tree printing. Karen, I thought, had simply forgotten to take her artist self to school. "It's only a public school class," she explained, "and this is the kind of stuff they expect from you! This is what I did when I was in school!" I couldn't help thinking, "Did you give your students a chance to find out what print making could be? Did they explore the possibilities? Was there something beautiful for them to see or hear, perhaps a recounting of your own printing discovery?" "That can't be done in the schools," Karen declared with certainty, after she had spent only five hours at her first teaching job.

I meet many teachers, in my graduate art education courses, who have sadly concluded that art and teaching don't mix. The first thing I say to them is that they were *not* naive or confused to dream of becoming both artists and teachers. There is nothing in the nature of either art or teaching that makes it impossible to combine these functions. The difficulty is in the tradition of art teaching, which requires them, as teachers, to do things and behave in ways that contradict the very nature of art, so that they can neither adequately teach art to their students nor find the stimulation they themselves need to function fully as artists. This tradition is often reinforced institutionally in the graduate schools and also in the public schools, where the importance and special nature of art as a subject have never been understood. Add to this the general lack of understanding of art among parents and others in the community, and one can see why individual art teachers may find no understanding of their situation and no support—and may see no way out.

Even the well-meant efforts of advocates of the arts to provide support for art in the schools by funding federal artist-in-residence programs has had a negative effect on art teachers. Unanimous praise for these projects has noted the visiting artist's ability to bring a "new creative spirit" to the schools. In many of the same schools, art is already being taught by dedicated teachers who work daily without similar funding and encouragement, fanfare, or administrative interest. Are they just "art teachers," while the artist-in-residence is a special kind of being? What so robs the spirit, confidence, and status of the teacher in the school that a "real" artist needs to be imported?

Many teachers are aware of their endangered situation but assume that help, if it ever comes, will have to come from above—from the federal government, the graduate schools, or the school systems. Until then, they plan to wait patiently—to "tough it out" as best they can. But there is no need to wait. The people who are really in a position to do the research in innovative art teaching are the art teachers in the classrooms—and even we have only just begun to explore our subject. The main obstacle to innovative teaching is not the lack of funding or community support: It is our own lack of self-confidence, and the fact that we have not learned to view ourselves as the primary scholars and researchers in our field.

How can individual teachers gain the self-confidence they need if they are to make a personal decision to begin experimenting with innovative teaching? Many of us work alone, without a support group of fellow artist-teachers and surrounded by parents, administrators, and other teachers who do not understand what is needed to bring art into the schools. Our education has taught us to look to others, particularly to specialists in education, for research and innovation. If we are to take on the new role of artist-teachers, we must learn to see ourselves in a new light: We must realize that the main responsibility for developing new educational theory and practice in art teaching, and for making sure that art in the schools keeps pace with art in the world, rests with us. As professional artists who work in school classrooms, we are the professionals in the best position to develop and test new educational theories in art education. Moreover, the nature of art requires that the theory of art education be developed by *individuals*, in a process of constant renewal, rather than being filtered down to the schools through *institutions*, in a process that promotes conformity, imitation, and stasis. The only thing that prevents us from functioning right now as the experts in our field is that we have not learned to view ourselves in that light.

We cannot afford to wait for others to come to our rescue. Not only are our students deprived of a real education in art by the present system; our own survival as artists and teachers is at stake. If we want to preserve our dreams of artistic achievement and fulfill our responsibility to our students, we must act. We have only to look around us to see that we are an endangered species: The present system can destroy both the artist and the teacher in the public schools.

Several kinds of awareness can give us the confidence we need to change the way art is taught. A major source of confidence is the knowledge that the essential preparation for art teaching is to be an artist. The ability to teach art does not depend on skills known primarily to specialists in education, but on precisely the skills that we have worked all our lives to perfect. Making an art lesson, as we have seen, requires exactly the same kind of ability to plan and previsualize that we use in making a work of art. We are skilled visual communicators, and visual—not verbal—communication skills are at the heart of art teaching. When we look around us in the schools and in the graduate schools, it is obvious that we artist-teachers, and we alone, are in the best position to become the experts in visual communication within the field of education. No one can speak with more authority in this area than we.

The realization that the teacher is the primary model of the artist for students will give us confidence by relieving us of guilt when we "take time from our teaching" (as we would formerly have described it) for our personal work. Once we have understood that the presence of a fully functioning artist in the classroom is essential to art teaching, the whole question of "teacher versus artist" appears in an entirely new perspective. Instead of *sacrificing* our art to our teaching, *giving up* the work we want to do to concern ourselves with the simplified art problems considered suitable for students, we take the opposite approach. We begin with the assumption that the serious artistic concerns of a professional artist are precisely the kinds of problems that apprentice artists need to learn about from us. We understand that the more time and effort we put into our personal work in art, the more knowledge and experience of art we will have to bring to our students. We are aware that we must function not just within the little world of the school but as members of the art world, not only for our own sakes but so that our students can learn, through us, about an artist's working life. Instead of struggling to separate the artist in us from the teacher, painfully deciding how much of our lives to give to each role, we will experience a new sense of wholeness as the formerly separate roles come together.

This will remove a serious source of tension in the lives of art teachers. Because we no longer have to leave our most cherished artistic plans and ideas at home when we go to school, we do not feel that our work in class is taking us away from our work in art, but that it is simply *part* of it. After all, our lessons are based on the ideas that we ourselves believe are most important about art, and our teaching is based on our own personal philosophy of art. When I teach a lesson that goes well I get the same feeling of total absorption of mind and body that I have while painting, and the satisfaction that I feel at the completion of such a lesson is like the satisfaction at the conclusion of a great art experience. Each successful lesson deepens my understanding of an art problem I want to explore and gives me new ideas for my artworks, as well as for future lessons.

Just as we experience teaching as part of our work in art, so we no longer perceive the time we spend on our own art as time taken away from preparing for our classes but, on the contrary, as essential *preparation* for art teaching. Lesson ideas come to us (just as art ideas do) while we are shopping or mowing the lawn or making art, and the more art projects we are intensely pursuing ourselves, the more lesson ideas we find. Besides selecting ideas to illustrate in detail in class, we feel free to share our latest discoveries with our students, whether or not they fit in with the day's lesson—taking a sample of a new color discovery in a plastic bag, for example, to show in class. We know that in sharing our work and our enthusiasm with our pupils, as we would with colleagues, we are not taking time away from "more important" matters or egotistically emphasizing our own work but, on the contrary, are performing a function vital to art teaching: creating an atmosphere of sharing, in which students learn, in turn, to share their own finds and their own genuine enthusiasms with each other and with us. We know that in letting children see something of our daily lives, we are helping them to understand artists as real people and are developing the kind of professionally responsible, yet personal, relationship with our students that is essential to all good teaching.

THE TEACHER AS MENTOR AND COLLEAGUE

Producing true art is a process of sharing. All creative acts are peformed in a spirit of giving part of oneself to another person, to a group of people, or to society at large. If students are to understand this, they must experience in art class the sense of belonging to a community in which everyone's contribution is valued and in which it is understood that everyone has something worthwhile to offer. If students are to risk exposing their real feelings and thoughts to others in art class, they need to experience there a totally caring and accepting environment. They need, especially, to be treated by the teacher with respect and kindness.

Our willingness to share something of our personal lives and art experiences with children is one of the ways in which we show respect for our students. When we tell children about our art ideas and our work, we are behaving as though we *assumed* that students can understand, and care about, the art ideas that interest an adult artist (and we do assume that). This is quite an unusual mark of respect, for few adults talk seriously and honestly with children about their interests and their work lives. Adults are more likely to offer children simplified versions of their experiences, considered more appropriate for children's supposedly limited understandings. Children immediately recognize the unusual quality of interchanges in which an adult is "leveling" with them and addressing them as equals, and the teacher's high opinion of them often gives them a better opinion of themselves and their own potential.

When the teacher shares art experiences with children, he or she becomes a model of the artist. The presentation of ourselves in this role is partly an intuitive act, but, because it is so important to art teaching, it also requires thought and planning. We must be aware of what sort of image we are presenting. Just going into class and "being yourself" is obviously not the idea, nor are all details from our personal lives appropriate for airing in class just because they are part of our lives. When we plan to reveal our own lives as artists to students, we are not on an ego trip, saying to students, "This approach to art is exciting because *I* do it!" On the contrary, as we consciously present the artist's role to our students, we approach it as an art form in which the teacher represents an art world of fundamental truths that transcends the teacher's self and personal interests. In "performing" the teacher's role or other dramatic roles for our students, our goal is not to draw attention to ourselves, but to get beyond the artist's individual ego, drawing attention *through* ourselves to the fundamental truths of art. What we are saying to students is, "I find art one of the most satisfying activities I have ever experienced, because *art* is so great." We do not try to tell students everything about ourselves, or bore them with trivia, or shock them just for the sake of excitement, but consciously select the events and experiences that we ourselves can see as representative of artists' lives and work styles.

Here is an example of some personal experiences from my own life that I told my students about in order to demonstrate that art ideas can occur anytime and anywhere. One day I arrived for my class wearing a hospital mask, with a stack of blue hospital pads under my arm, operating-room shoe covers on my feet, and a roll of paper tapes in my hand. After making my dramatic entrance in this costume, I began setting up the table at the front of the room with a tablecloth, napkins, cups, and hats all decorated with a Star Wars design. I entitled my lecture "I did not forget about you" (meaning the class).

Then I began to explain to my students that this had been a memorable week in my life. The major event was the birth of my third child, at which I assisted in the hospital. I described how, while I was helping my wife with the breathing exercises in the labor room, I became interested in the tape of graph paper and the mechanical drawing tools that were being used to record the baby's heartbeat and my wife's contractions. I also noted that the blue padded sheet that the nurse had put on the bed matched the color of the disposable paper masks and shoe covers that the staff and I wore. The students were intrigued as I explained that in spite of my involvement in the intensely emotional experience of watching the baby's birth, and in spite of my concern for my wife, I still couldn't help noticing these things that looked interesting for work in art and took care to collect samples to bring to class. In fact, because of the excitement and the unfamiliar setting of the labor room, my creative senses were all the more alive, and I was especially sensitive to possibilities for art lessons and art-works.

The second important event of my week, I explained, had been my son's eight-year-old birthday party, which I had organized. It was designed as the ultimate Star Wars event, complete with a Star Wars cake, tablecloth, napkins, cups, and hats. This too intrigued the class, and we went on to use the sparklers, balloons, bubbles, and confetti from the birthday party that I had also brought along as the subject of paintings.

In a subsequent lesson, I described how at the hospital the doctors had carried around white patient folders with long strips of electrocardiogram tapes clipped inside and how, when our own physician walked in, the long strips of tape were gently unfolding and hanging out of his folder. The sight of these mechanical drawings hanging from the white folder stayed with me, and I proceeded to explore a whole series of "folder drawings," using a folder with long white strips of paper on which I executed my drawings. I brought ten of these folder drawings to class. We talked about ways to package such drawings using envelopes, trays, bags, or pockets, and the possibility of doing drawings in containers, which led later to the students' collecting their own containers on which to draw. I tried not merely to give an assignment that copied my experience but one that illuminated its source, so that broader concepts could be developed.

The techniques for managing conversations about art and about student projects that were described earlier in this book are also ways of expressing respect for students and of developing a relationship based on trust and liking. Instead of lecturing or giving directions, the teacher's stance is that of a fellow investigator—someone who is constantly curious, constantly asking questions, but reluctant to provide answers or judgments; someone who is always learning, and is happy to learn from and *with* the students. This does not mean that teachers cannot express what they know, but that we express it, and guide students' explorations, primarily through sensitive questioning and comments that make connections among art ideas rather than through instructions or criticisms. In all of our comments, our words and tone of voice should be caring and loving. This is especially important when we are responding to students' plans for their projects, explanations of their art ideas and feelings, and their finished works. When students find that their perceptions and thoughts (which they may not dare to value much themselves) seem worthwhile and interesting to the teacher, they may be encouraged to trust the teacher with more of their inner visions. They may also begin to value their own perceptions and feelings more highly, and as a result become more interested in pursuing and expressing them.

My daughter, at one point in her elementary school years, had difficulty with her school subjects. She managed to maintain her confidence in herself by letting everyone know that her ideas were so great that her dad constantly took notes on them. Particular attention to children's ideas through actually writing them down in front of the student certifies that one's idea is a truly valuable commodity.

Perhaps the following anecdote will illustrate the attitude of acceptance of children's values and feelings that I am trying to describe. One day an artist friend of mine came to visit me, with his young daughter. There had been a heavy rainstorm that morning, but by the time they arrived the sky had cleared, the sun had come out, the puddles had dried up, and it was a beautiful day. The little girl still had her plastic umbrella with her, though, and apparently her mind was still on how much fun it would be to use her umbrella in the rain. She said to her father, "Can we go out and play in the rain?" Instead of reminding her (as many parents would have) that the rain had stopped, my friend said, "Okay, let's have a run in the rain! You put up your umbrella, and I'll run through the puddles!" Out they went, and the dancing pair was delightful to watch as they played in the imaginary rain and skipped through fantasized puddles. Art teachers show the same kind of care and understanding that my friend showed for his daughter when they accept and share children's dreams and ideas and help them to build their art on the excitement of exploring the environment, whether it is the rain, the breeze, a new umbrella, a real or an imaginary puddle.

All of the students in the class must feel that their ideas are valued by the teacher. For this reason it is important to avoid designating certain students as "class artists" or attempting to mold a few selected pupils after our own style or image. We should try, during each lesson, to give our full attention at some point to each member of the class, responding to the student on the basis of individual need rather than presenting ideas or formulas to be used by everyone. When students find that the teacher wants to hear about their art ideas, as well as telling about his or her own, they begin to experience the interaction in the class as sharing. The teacher's example of a positive, friendly, accepting response to students' ideas and their artworks—rather than a critical, judgmental stance—is also a powerful example to the students to be supportive of each other. Gradually students realize that competition is out of place in art class; that through art you can express yourself in a satisfying way while, at the same time, you give something of value to others.

A teacher's willingness to play with students, to be silly (wearing funny hats, telling jokes, describing absurd and fantastic visions, dancing, and other unexpected behaviors), is also a way of showing respect for children's attitudes and interests. Here again, as in sharing details of our personal lives, teachers set the example of self-revelation for the children. If teachers dare to reveal the part of themselves that is playful, imaginative, and "silly" (by conventional standards), the children too may dare to play and to reveal their far-out visions and dreams. Real involvement and genuine self-revelation are essential for art making, but we cannot expect children to share their fragile feelings and dreams, which are so often roughly handled in school by teachers and students alike, unless we ourselves are willing to take the same risk.

Although some teachers fear that such an informal teaching style will lead to a loss of authority, I have not found this to be so. When we make it possible for children to relax in class and become personally involved in their work, so that they feel its value for themselves, they are far more willing to cooperate and to behave responsibly. If we succeed in letting students in on the secret of what art has to offer them, they begin to *want* to be artists—and to want to imitate the teacher. The rewards of treating students as fellow artists are well worth any temporary discomfort that an experienced teacher may feel in adjusting to a new teaching style. Our students, precisely because they are children, have original ideas and fresh observations to offer that can help us to get beyond our established notions and discover new worlds. Sharing great art ideas and images of visual beauty may then become an everyday occurrence, and instead of feeling ourselves isolated in a school, with only a rare student-artist or two to share the art experience, we may find ourselves where we always wanted to be: in a community of artists.

Afterword

When artists become teachers in the public schools, they are expected to blend into a public school system that is run according to arbitrary routines and regulations, and are faced with a community that holds art in low esteem. In bringing art to the schools, we therefore must understand our task to include not only students but parents, colleagues, and communities. Instead of blending in and becoming invisible, we must make art highly visible, so that parents and staff members in the school can share the excitement of children's art making and also understand our experimental teaching.

In 1980, with the aid of funding from our state arts council, I decided to try such an approach in the public schools in Lexington, Kentucky. The program is still vital and has served twenty-four area schools. The Adopt-A-School project was developed to support the delicate process of transferring the artistic process to the community by allowing future teachers (under the direction of an experienced teacher) to try out innovations in art teaching in the schools, instead of permitting all of the important problems to be simplified, foolproofed, and prejudged in university classes before they reached the classroom.

In the Adopt-A-School program, a room or space is provided at the host school, where art education students examine the theory and practice of their field, as well as creating artworks that the school community is invited to view. This is followed by practice teaching in which the future teachers apply their learning, working with the children under the watchful eyes of the college supervisor and the school staff. This program has provided many of the firsthand experiences discussed in this book.

I set up the program because I believe that if college art teaching is to bring change to the public schools, we must devise a more efficient system of filtering down change than simply waiting for future art teachers to be placed. Innovations need to be brought closer to the schools, showcased within them, and supported in their infancy by all concerned. Art teachers who spend their days supporting student innovations need support themselves if they are to have the confidence to introduce future innovations. I have found that working each day in the schools themselves with children, future teachers, and school staff, within close view of the parents, is the most promising avenue for bringing about change. All of the affected parties in the school must be brought together if art innovations are to blossom, rather than wilting, when they are carried from teacher-training institutions to the school system.

As I pointed out at the beginning, this book is not intended as a formula or prescription for art teaching, but rather as a description of my own experience in art teaching that I hope will encourage other art teachers to write their own books. Let me end, then, by saying that every art teacher must write a book. Don't be scared, dear reader! What I mean is that art teachers have great ideas, that creative ideas are the substance of their work, and that these ideas need to be taken seriously, written down, and prized. Art teaching needs to be built by the art teachers in the schools, all of them making their own experiments. "Research" (that forbidding term that sounds so formal) in art education really ought to be just a matter of teachers sharing with each other the discoveries that we make in our classrooms—not something that we leave up to those who teach at the college level. We are the real experts in this field. All of us make unique discoveries as we teach— and that is why each of us can write a book.

Because we were trained as visual communicators, rather than as verbal communicators, artists often feel that writing is foreign to them and that they lack the skills to do it. It took me many years to realize that writing (for art teachers) is simply recording the good ideas we have, and that research in our field is simply the ability to observe, interpret, and organize ideas that artists are already comfortable with. This book, like an artwork, was developed from ideas recorded in many idea- and sketchbooks and from observations and discoveries made in actual teaching situations. Some of it was originally written on the back of an old drawing and on the label of a paint jar—in other words, it developed from notes taken everywhere and jotted down quickly, sometimes in strange places, not from a formal process of sitting down and writing (although some of that was needed later). Although we work in separate schools, scattered in many different parts of the country, as we make our experiments with teaching we are engaged in a communal process, and we need to communicate the results to each other so that we can learn from and encourage each other.

If you began reading this book with the assumption that only art teachers in colleges and graduate schools can write on our subject, perhaps you will end it by starting to think about writing your own book about art teaching. I hope you will select a notebook and start making your notes for it today: I'm anxious to read *your* book!

Appendix A:

Content of Conversation
in Art Classes

Because in my observations of art classes I had found little conversation of substance between art teachers and their students—exchanges that related to the nature of art or to the processes of art as observed or experienced by children—I decided to examine examples of art teaching through a series of tape recordings of art lessons and to analyze the interchanges between students and teachers.

ART-RELATED AND NON-ART-RELATED CONVERSATION

Over an eight-month period, I tape-recorded twenty-seven art classes held by nine different teachers (three sessions were recorded for each teacher). The teachers were randomly selected from an urban school district, and the experiment focused on grades 5, 6, and 7, an overlap between elementary and middle school. The taping was done by student teachers with the consent of the cooperating teachers, who themselves selected the lessons to be taped. The tapes were coded at one-minute intervals according to two major categories: art-related conversation and non-art-related conversation. Each of these categories was divided into five subcategories. *Art-related conversation* was about:

1. *Art vocabulary*: definitions, names of tools, techniques, artists, and so forth.
2. *Art materials*: their distribution, location, and availability; the nature of their use, and so on.
3. *Media and techniques*: instructions and guidelines on how to use materials, safety tips, and the like.

4. *Art demonstrations*: techniques, media, use of tools, materials, and processes.
5. *The creative process*: discussion of artists' or students' work, ideas, and reactions to art experiences.

Non-art-related conversation was about:

1. *Attendance taking*: anything concerned with attendance, such as hall passes, office notices, and tardiness.
2. *General school announcements*: changes in school scheduling, ball games, and so on.
3. *Classroom maintenance*: cleanup instructions, hanging up coats, putting away books or art supplies, and the like.
4. *Discipline problems*: warnings, instructions, or actions related to classroom behavior.
5. *Current events*: boy- or girlfriends, the weather, and so forth.

An analysis of the tapes showed that non-art-related areas took up 68 percent of the classroom conversation. For example, in the twenty-seven sessions taped, references to the art-related conversations' category no. 5 occurred only six times, and even then only in short, improvised statements. At the beginning and the end of the period, when the teachers dealt primarily with routines and classroom management, the conversation related to art only 8 percent of the time. There were seldom adequate explanations of why the students were to do a particular lesson; where the teacher's idea for the lesson came from, or what inspired it; how the lesson related to the art world or to the interests of the children; or how or what the children might contribute to the lesson. There were very few instances of the children's speaking of their own ideas or sharing their plans and visions with the class or the teacher. There were even fewer discussions of the children's reactions to their own art making, to their accomplishments and difficulties in creation.

The teachers gave a number of reasons for these results, which can be summarized as follows:

1. The time for working in the class period is very short, so that the introduction to a lesson has to be short and to-the-point, and the end of the period has to be devoted to cleanup.
2. Talking before or during the class work is apt to distract the children and to confuse them about the teacher's original intent for the lesson.

3. The children are too young and unsophisticated to benefit from any meaningful discussion of art.

As a result, the art class consists, aside from routine and managerial matters, of the teacher's assigning a quite specific task and the children's carrying it out according to rather limiting instructions. Very little attempt is made to encourage the student's originality or independence. Nor are the children encouraged to think of art as something that extends outside the classroom as a part of everyday life, to relate themselves and what they are doing to the art world, or to think of themselves as possible future artists.

Appendix B:

Printed Resources

Sample Books
New and antique wallpapers, buttons, tiles, fabrics, paints, car interiors

Charts and Maps
Fashion patterns, antique maps, eye charts, anatomy charts, dance charts, city and landscaping plans, X-rays, computer-coded maps, electronic circuits, parts and wiring diagrams, assembling instructions

Catalogs
Cooking and baking catalogs—e.g., Maid of Scandinavia
Drafting and office suppliers—e.g., Koh-I-Noor
Toy catalogs—e.g., Childcraft, Community Playthings, FAO Schwartz, Just for Kids, Novo Toys, Tinkertoy Idea Book
Model train catalogs—e.g., Marklin, Lionel
Plant and garden catalogs—e.g., Burpee Seed Company
Fashion catalogs—e.g., Lord and Taylor, Bonwit Teller, Saks Fifth Avenue
Museum gift shop catalogs—e.g., Museum of Modern Art, Museum of Natural History
Fabric catalogs—e.g., F. Schumacher
Plumbing supply catalogs—e.g., American Standard, Kohler
Tents and outdoor equipment catalogs—e.g., Harrison's Camping Supplies
Scientific supply catalogs—e.g., Edmonton Scientific, Radio Shack
Guinness Book of World Records

Magazines
Smithsonian, National Geographic, Architectural Digest, Sesame Street, Interior Design, L'Officiel, Art News, Art Forum, Life, and old collectible issues of all kinds of magazines with interesting illustrations, e.g., *Mad Magazine,* comics

Plan and Idea Books
Artist's sketchbooks, poet's doodle books, choreographer's drawing and notation books, composer's day books, architect's presentation books, engineer's notebooks, scientist's lab books, fashion designer's illustrations, cartoonist's idea and plan books, art teacher's plan books

Throw-aways
New and old theater tickets, coupons, stamps, restaurant place mats, menus, receipts, letters, children's toy boxes, packages, brochures, shopping bags, gift boxes, wrappers, napkin collections

Posters
New and old product posters, posters showing rock stars and super-heroes, performance and film posters, billboard sections and show posters

Children's Books
New and old alphabet books, pop-up books, coloring books, comic books, poetry books, activity books, book jackets

Game Boards
New and old puzzles, mazes, board games, targets, pinball machines

Memorabilia
Class photos, family albums, films, report cards, scrapbooks, diplomas, marriage certificates, autographs, letters

Identification Cards
Old and new student ID cards, workplace ID cards, prison ID cards, fingerprint charts, ID photos

Play Cards
Old and new counting cards, Old Maid decks, Barbie doll cards, play cards of the 50 states, animal cards, bubble gum cards, cards of rock stars, Garbage Pail Kids, baseball cards

Photographs
Polaroid and other photos of places and people, stereo cards, shadow-graphs, holography examples, time-lapse photos, photo-micro-graphs, reproductions of computer art, family albums

Postcards
New and old valentines, postcards from cities, country fairs, and other places of interest, museum cards, greeting cards

Store Advertisements
New and old calendars, fans, fast-food giveaways, children's "Happy Meals" hats and restaurant menus, paper birthday crowns, sale brochures

Labels
New and old food can labels, clothing labels, key and shipping tags, stickers, decals, boxes with lettering or illustrations, postal labels, notary labels, price labels, shipping labels

Cutouts
Old and new stencils, punch-outs, foldouts, cutout dolls, cut-out paper rooms and cities

Appendix C:

Shopping Sources

Truck stops (for truck mirrors, souvenirs, hats)

Gift shops at the museum, zoo, or amusement park (for gift and souvenir cards, toys)

Used book stores (for old children's books, catalogs, medical charts)

Greeting card stores (for 3-D cards, musical cards, cards with liquids and smells)

Theatrical makeup and costume rentals (for unusual masks, makeup and brushes)

Toy stores (for blocks, game boards, art toys, plastic figures)

Antique stores and flea markets (for old buttons, signs, costume jewelry)

Thrift shops (for old appliances, hats, suitcases)

Diners and restaurants (for place mats, menus, table advertisements, matchboxes)

Fabric stores (for laces, Velcro, tracing wheels, rulers)

Government surplus and Army, Navy stores (for parachutes, flashlights, helmets)

Fast-food restaurants (for food packaging, giveaways, place mats)

Contemporary furnishings stores (for hooks, hangers, folding chairs, plastic ware)

Art-supply stores (for metallic markers, Day-Glo chalks, spray glitter)

Bakeries (for decorated cookies, oddly shaped rolls, cake decorating tools)

Home improvement centers (for insulation materials, tapes, fasteners, unusual light bulbs)

Wholesale paper goods and restaurant party suppliers (for party favors, key tags, party prizes)

Automotive parts stores (for funnels, car cleaning mitts, retouching colors)

Kitchen equipment stores (for mixing containers, basters, baking mitts, large spoons)

Supermarkets (for scrub brushes, napkins, labels, display racks, six-packs)

Plumbing supply stores (for plastic and copper pipes, silver tape, tools)

Wholesale florist supplies (for florist tapes, wires, ferns, wrapping papers)

Janitorial supplies (for mops, sponges, dispensers)

Sporting goods stores (for fishing lures, swim goggles, ski boot catalogs)

Chocolate factories (for molds, wrappers, boxes, candy-making sticks)

Bibliography

The Artist

Bourgeois, Louise. *Louise Bourgeois*. New York: The Museum of Modern Art, 1982.

Flam, Jack D. *Matisse on Art*. New York: E. P. Dutton, 1978.

Hedgecoe, John, and Moore, Henry. *Henry Moore*. New York: Simon & Schuster, 1968.

Herbert, Robert L. *Modern Artists on Art*. Englewood Cliffs, N.J.: Prentice-Hall, 1964.

Lartigue, Jacques Henri. *Diary of a Century*. New York: Viking Press, 1970.

Lord, James. *A Giacommetti Portrait*. New York: The Museum of Modern Art, 1964.

Lyons, Nathan. *Photographers on Photography*. Englewood Cliffs, N.J.: Prentice-Hall, 1966.

Rodman, Selden. *Conversations with Artists*. New York: Capricorn Books, 1961.

Rose, Barbara. *Claes Oldenburg*. New York: The Museum of Modern Art, 1970.

Salomon, Charlotte. *Charlotte: Life or Theater*. New York: Viking Press, 1981.

Wye, Deborah. *Louise Bourgeois*. New York: Museum of Modern Art, 1982.

Play

Copple, C., Spiegel, I., and Sanders, R. *Educating the Young Thinker: Classroom Strategies for Cognitive Growth*. New York: Van Nostrand, 1979.

Feigenbaum, Mitchel, and Feder, B. "Inventing the future." *New York Times Magazine*, May 19, 1984, pp. 6–9.

Gordon, Alice Kaplan. *Games for Growth*. Chicago: Science Research Associates, 1972.

Hanimals. La Jolla, Calif.: The Green Tiger Press, 1982.

Hartley, Ruth E. *Children's Play*. New York: Thomas Y. Crowell, 1963.

Kaprow, Allen. *Assemblages, Environments and Happenings*. New York: Abrams Publishing, 1966.

King, Martha. *Informal Learning*. Bloomington, Ind.: Phi Delta Kappa, 1974.

Slade, Peter. *Child Drama.* London: University of London Press, 1954.
———. *Experience of Spontaneity.* London: Longman, 1969.
Tassel, Katrina, and Freimann, Millie. *Creative Dramatization.* New York: Macmillan, 1973.

Visual Communication

Arnheim, Rudolf. *Visual Thinking.* Berkeley, Calif.: University of California Press, 1969.
Barlund, D. C. *Interpersonal Communications.* Boston, Mass.: Houghton Mifflin, 1978.
Chaet, Bernard. *An Artist's Notebook.* New York: Holt, Rinehart and Winston, 1979.
Heger, H. K. *Verbal and Nonverbal Classroom Communication.* Minneapolis, Minn.: Paper delivered at the Annual Meeting of the American Educational Research Association, 1975. (ERIC Document Reproduction Service No. ED 040 975)
Hinkle, J. E. *Evaluation and Nonverbal Techniques.* Fort Collins, Colo.: Colorado State University, 1976. (ERIC Document Reproduction Service No. ED 033 412)
Rees, W., and Ruesch, J. *Non-verbal Communication.* Berkeley, Calif.: University of California Press, 1956.

Line

Aero, Rita. *New Technology Coloring Book.* New York: Bantam Books, 1983.
Blaser, Werner. *Folding Chairs.* Stuttgart, Germany: Birkhauser, 1982.
Calder, Alexander. *Calder's Circus.* New York: E. P. Dutton, 1972.
Cirker, Blanche. *Needlework Designs.* New York: Dover Press, 1975.
Evans, Larry. *Three Dimensional Mazes.* San Francisco: Troubador Press, 1979.
Fairbank, A. *A Book of Scripts.* London: Penguin, 1960.
Feder, Norman. *Art of the East Plains Indians.* New York: The Brooklyn Museum, 1964.
Finch, Christopher. *Walt Disney.* New York: Harry Abrams, 1973.
Franke, H. W. *Computer Graphics, Computer Art.* London: Phaidon, 1971.
Friedlander, Lee. *Self Portrait.* New York: Haywire Press, 1970.
Graham, W. *Paul Klee—Drawings.* New York: Harry Abrams, 1960.
Green, Gerald. *The Artists of Terezin.* New York: Shocken Books, 1970.
Krueger, Glee. *A Gallery of American Samplers.* New York: Museum of American Folk Art, 1978.
Steinberg, Saul. *The Passport.* New York: Random House, 1979.
Stevens, John. *Zen and the Art of Calligraphy.* London: Routledge & Kegan Paul, 1983.
Termini, Benedict. *Essentials of Echocardiography.* Union, N.J.: Oradell Press, 1982.

Color

Bennett, Ian. *Carpets of the World.* New York: A. & W. Publishing Co., 1977.

Compton, Michael. *Pop Art.* New York: Paul Hamlyn, 1970.

Cooper, Marsha. *Subway Art.* New York: Holt, Rinehart & Winston, 1985.

Demur, Guy. *Staell.* New York: Crown, 1955.

Edwards, D. *Painted Walls of Mexico.* Austin: University of Texas Press, 1966.

Eggleston, William. *William Eggleston's Guide.* New York: Museum of Modern Art, 1976.

Elderfield, John. *The Cut-outs of Henri Matisse.* New York: George Braziller, 1978.

Haas, Ernest. *Venice: The Great Cities.* New York: Time-Life Books, 1976.

Haders, Phyllis. *Sunshine and Shadow: The Amish and Their Quilts.* New York: Universe Books, 1976.

Huyghe, Renee. *Byzantine and Medieval Art.* New York: Paul Hamlyn, 1958.

Mack, Kathy. *American Neon.* New York: Universe Books, 1976.

Form

Ayliffe, Jerry. *Jukeboxes.* Florence, Ala.: Books Americana, 1985.

Dawes, Nicholas. *Lalique Glass.* New York: Crown, 1986.

DeThier, Jean. *Down to Earth: Sandforms.* New York: Facts on File, Inc. 1981.

Feininger, Andreas. *Shells, Forms and Designs of the Sea.* New York: Dover Press, 1983.

Flether, Edward. *Antique Bottles.* London: Blandford Press, 1976.

Fraley, Tobin. *The Carousel Animal.* Berkeley, Calif.: Zephyr Press, 1983.

Fuller, B. *Noguchi.* New York: Harper & Row, 1968.

Gordon, Archie. *Towers.* London: David & Charles, 1979.

Hatton, E. M. *The Tent Book.* Boston: Houghton Mifflin, 1979.

Hennessey, William. *Russel Wright American Designer.* Cambridge: M.I.T. Press, 1983.

Rasmussen, Steein Eiler. *Experiencing Architecture.* Cambridge: M.I.T. Press, 1959.

Schiffer, Nancy. *Baskets.* Exton, Pa.: Schiffer, 1984.

Wye, Deborah. *Louise Bourgeois.* New York: Museum of Modern Art, 1982.

The Environment

Bennett, George. *Mannequins.* New York: Alfred Knopf, 1977.

Cartier-Bresson, Henry. *The World of Henry Cartier-Bresson.* New York: Viking Press, 1968.

Davidson, Bruce. *East 100 Street.* Cambridge: Harvard University Press, 1970.

Krims, Les. *Little People of America.* Los Angeles: Folio Press, 1972.

Liberman, William S. *Manhattan Observed.* New York: The Museum of Modern Art, 1968.

Mead, Margaret, and Heyman, Ken. *Family.* New York: Macmillan, 1965.

Nagy, Moholy L. *Vision in Motion*. Chicago: Paul Theobald, 1947.

Schaffer, Richard. *Hotel: Casinos of Las Vegas*. Danbury, Conn.: Archives Press, 1974.

Schneider, Ira, and Korot, Beryl. *Video Art*. New York: Harcourt Brace Jovanovich, 1976.

Szekely, George. *A Study of a Community—Staten Island Architecture and Environment*. Staten Island, N.Y.: The Staten Island Continuum of Education, 1980.

Thiebaud, Wayne. *Wayne Thiebaud*. Seattle: University of Washington Press, 1985.

Woolston, Bill. *Iowa Fair*. Genesee, Idaho: Thorn Creek Press, 1975.

Collecting

Baker, Lillian. *Collectible Jewelry*. Peducah, Ky.: Collector's Books, 1985.

Bertoia, Jeanne. *Doorstops*. Peducah, Ky.: Collector's Books, 1985.

Blaser, Verneer. *Folding Chairs*. Basel, Switzerland: Birkhauser Verlag, 1982.

Bosker, Gideon. *Great Shakes: Salt and Pepper Shakers*. New York: Abbeville Press, 1986.

Delano, Sharon. *Texas Boots*. New York: Penguin Books, 1981.

Dittrick, Mark. *The Bed Book*. New York: Harcourt Brace Jovanovich, 1980.

Karolewitz, T. *This Was Trucking*. New York: Bonanza, 1972.

Kron, J. *High Tech*. New York: Clarkson N. Potter, 1978.

Miles, Charles. *Indian and Eskimo Artifacts*. New York: Bonanza, 1970.

Nondness, L. *Objects U. S. A.* New York: Viking Press, 1970.

Rowland, Amy. *Handcrafted Doors and Windows*. Harrisburg, Pa.: Rodale Press, 1982.

Whitmyer, Margaret. *Hall China*. Peducah, Ky.: Collector's Books, 1984.

Printed Works

Black, Mary. *American Advertising Posters of the Nineteenth Century*. New York: Dover, Inc., 1976.

Braque, Georges. *Georges Braque: His Graphic Works*. New York: Harry Abrams, 1961.

Jewett, K. *Early New England Wall Stencils*. New York: Harmony Books, 1979.

Kovel, Ralph, and Kovel, Terry. *The Kovels Book of Antique Labels*. New York: Crown, 1982.

Marsh, R. *Monoprints*. London: Tiranti, 1969.

Morse, P. *Etchings by John Sloan*. St. Louis: University of Missouri Press, 1967.

Rhodes, Zandra, and Knight, Anne. *The Art of Zandra Rhodes*. New York: Houghton Mifflin, 1985.

Sadowsky, N. *The Prints of Reginald Marsh*. New York: Clarkson N. Potter, 1976.

Singer, I., and Frasconi, A. *Elijah the Slave*. New York: Farrar, Straus, & Giroux, 1970.
Spies, Werner. *Max Ernst Frottages*. New York: Thames & Hudson, 1986.

Toys

Buhler, Michael. *Tin Toys 1945–1975*. New York: Fox, 1976.
Fox, D. *The Doll*. New York: Harry Abrams, 1978.
Friedberg, P. *Handcrafted Playgrounds*. New York: Random House, 1975.
Hannas, Linda. *The Jigsaw Book: Jigsaw Puzzling Around the World*. New York: Dial Press, 1981.
Kitahara. *Toy Robots*. San Francisco: Chronicle, 1985.
Mandel, Margaret. *Teddy Bears and Steif Animals*. Peducah, Ky.: Collector's Books, 1984.
Ness, E. *Cut-out Interiors from the Metropolitan Museum of Art*. New York: The Metropolitan Museum of Art, 1977.
Wendel, Bruce. *Gameboards of North America*. New York: E. P. Dutton, 1986.

Children's Books

Asch, Frank. *George's Store*. New York: Charles Scribner & Sons, 1972.
Mayer, Mercer. *East of the Sun and West of the Moon*. New York: Four Winds Press, 1980.
Meggendorfer, Lothar. *The City Park: A Reproduction of an Antique Stand-up Book*. New York: The Metropolitan Museum of Art, 1985.
Meggendorfer, Lothar. *International Circus: A Reproduction of an Antique Pop-up Book*. New York: Penguin Books, 1979.
Miller, Jonathan. *The Human Body*. New York: Viking Press, 1983.
Pienkowski, Jan. *Haunted House Pop-up Book*. New York: E. P. Dutton, 1979.
Rey, H. A. *Curious George Learns the Alphabet*. Boston: Houghton Mifflin, 1963.
Sendak, Maurice. *In the Night Kitchen*. New York: Harper & Row, 1970.
Seuss, Dr. *The Butter Battle Book*. New York: Random House, 1985.
Szekely, George. *Children's Books in the School Art Program*. Washington, D.C.: National Art Education Association, 1986.
Voigt, Erna. *Peter and the Wolf*. Boston: David Gordine, 1980.

General

Diemert, H. "The Problem of Content in Art Education." *Art Education*, 33, no. 7 (1980): 28–29.
Fiedler, Conrad. *On Judging Works of Art*. Berkeley, Calif.: University of California Press, 1969.
Gardner, Howard. *The Arts and Human Development*. New York: John Wiley & Sons, 1973.

Gardner, Howard, and Winner, Ellen. "How Children Learn: States of Understanding Art." *Psychology Today* (March 1976): 42–48.

Hurwitz, Al. *Programs of Promise: Art in the Schools*. New York: Harcourt Brace Jovanovich, 1972.

Mattli, Edward L. *The self in art education*. Washington, D.C.: National Art Education Association, Monograph no. 5, 1972.

McFee, J., and Degge, S. *Art, Culture and Environment: A Catalyst for Teaching*. Belmont, Calif.: Wadsworth, 1977.

Mills, E. *In the Suzuki Style: Ways to Encourage Children Musically*. Berkeley, Calif.: Diablo Press, 1974, pp. 7–39.

Plummer, Gordon A. *Children's Art Judgment*. Dubuque, Iowa: William C. Brown, 1974.

Read, Herbert. *Education Through Art*. London: Faber & Faber, 1975.

Silverman, Ronald. *A Syllabus for Art Education*. Los Angeles: California State University, 1976.

Taunton, Martha. "Reflective Dialogue in the Art Classroom: Focusing on the Art Process." *Art Education* 37 (January 1984): 15–17.

Index

Abstract expressionism, 14
Adopt-A-School program, 173–74
Antiques, 59
Arbus, Diane, 129–30
Architectural studies, 49, 134–35
Art books, 59–61
Art ideas
  arrangement of classroom space
    and, 62
  color and, 83–85
  experimentation in, 4, 6, 43–44,
    70–72
  exploration of, 14–15
  form and, 85–89
  found objects and, 14–15, 88
  importance of searching for,
    29–30
  importance of thinking about, 4
  inter-artist communication of, 19,
    140–42, 146–47
  for lesson plans, 97–102
  line and, 67, 75–78, 81–83
  materials as source of, 34–37
  movement and, 78–83
  performance by teacher and,
    91–96
  placement of materials in
    classroom and, 54–55
  planning in development of, 26–27
  play and, 25–26, 69–70, 75, 102–3
  shopping as source of, 30–33,
    111–13
  show-and-tell sessions as source
    of, 37, 53, 133
  sketchbooks and generation of,
    38–43, 98, 103, 120–21

sources of, 11–13, 19–20, 30–31,
    106–15
  student selection of, 6–7
  teacher selection of, 6–7
  teaching in development of, 9–11
  transformation in, 69–70, 136–37
  verbalization of, 140, 143–46
  visual evaluation of, 146
Artists
  characteristics of, 17–18
  as "gallery owners," 153, 155–58
  nonconformity of, 66, 131
  sharing of ideas among, 19,
    140–42, 146–47
  stereotypes concerning, 18–19
  student knowledge of, 60–61,
    124–25
  teachers as, 91, 161–66
  time management and, 44–45,
    115–18
  use of sketchbooks by, 40–43, 98,
    103
Art supplies, 112
Art teachers. *See* Teachers
Artworks, 59–61
Audience-participation formats,
    157

Bags, 57, 86
Ballpoint pens, 49
Block play, 49, 134–35
Body parts, 71
  linear play and, 77
  movement play based on, 79–83
  print making and, 82–83

Books, 57
  art, 59–61
  as source of art ideas, 114–15
Brushes, 30–31
Buttons, 57

Camera, 39
Canvas, 14–15
Caricature, 101
Catalogs, 32–33, 57, 59
  as source of art ideas, 113
Celebrations, 128–29
Charts, 57
Choreography, 15–16
Classroom characteristics, 47–96
  design of room, 50, 61–67, 104
  display of art, 50, 55–61
  material design and, 50, 51–55
  play and, 51, 67–89
  teaching as performance and, 51,
    89–96
Clothing, 57, 69, 92, 93, 136–37
Collections, 56, 57–59, 67
Color
  collections based on, 67
  in play, 67, 83–85, 93
Commercial art, 31–32, 86–87
Comparisons and contrasts, 101–2
Conclusions, lesson, 126–32
Contemporary art
  attention to objects in, 9
  basic nature of, 7–9
  environmental search and, 29
  experience in, 15
  importance of art ideas in, 9–11
  multimedia experiences in, 16
  role of choreography in, 15–16
  setups in, 13–14, 109
  subjects of, 7–8, 11–14
  trying the artist's role in, 1, 16–20
Contrasts and comparisons, 101–2
Conversation
  content of typical classroom,
    177–79

  in imaginative play, 73
  inter-artist, 19, 140–42, 146–47
  planning for art discussion, 122–24
  teacher-student, 166–67, 169
Costumes, 57, 69, 92, 93, 136–37
Covers, 57, 150
Crayon, 34
Cutting apart and placing together,
  150

Dance, 80–83, 94
Decision making, teacher versus
  student, 3–7
Diagramming, 149
Dishes, 57
Displays, 86, 92, 124–25
  of art objects and works of art,
    50, 55–61
  of completed art works in class,
    140
  formal exhibits, 153–59
  of found items in classroom,
    52–55
Dolls, 57
Drama, 72
  self-evaluation through, 147–48
Drawing
  dance as preliminary play for, 81
  lack of encouragement for, 47–49
  in lesson planning, 104
  line, 75–76
  linear play and, 77
  movement and, 78
  penmanship versus, 49, 76, 81
  redrawing, 128
  in self-evaluation, 149–50
  sources of art ideas for, 31
Dressing up play, 136–37
Drums, 81

Ehrlich, Robbie, 64
Elaboration, 151–52
Enlargement, 151

Environment
  as art supply store, 28
  materials research and, 28, 52–54,
    112–15
  relationship of forms to, 86
  shopping as method of exploring,
    30–33
  as source of art ideas, 28
  as source of lesson ideas, 111–15
  ways to encourage search of,
    52–54
Estimating, 150–51
Evaluation
  of lesson, as work of art, 132–33
  self-. *See* Self-evaluation
Exhibits, 153–59
  "gallery-owner" approach to, 153,
    155–58
  importance of, 158–59
  student observation of
    professional, 153, 154–55
  as tools for student learning, 153,
    154
  unusual approaches to design of,
    156–58
Experimentation
  importance of, 4, 6, 43–44
  preliminary play and, 70–72
Extenders of vision, 57, 61
Eyeglasses, 61

Fabric design, 95–96
Fantasy
  movement and, 80
  in play, 71, 72–75, 102–3
Field trips, 1
Finished works
  exhibits of, 153–59
  self-evaluation of. *See* Self-
    evaluation
  sketchbooks in assessment of, 41
Floors
  alteration of classroom, 65
  classroom display areas on, 53–54

Food
  collections of, 57, 59
  play with, 92
  as source of art ideas, 31
Form
  play and, 87–89
  study and observation of, 85–87
Found items
  in contemporary art, 13–14
  form and, 88
  in home art, 109
  shopping to locate, 30–33, 111–13
  show-and-tell sessions for, 37, 53
  sources of, 53
  storage and display of, 52–55
Framing, 151
Furniture, 66

Games, 129. *See also* Play
Gloves, 58, 111–12
Goal-setting, 142–43
Graffiti, 47
Group activities
  role of, 25–26
  show-and-tell sessions, 37, 53, 133
  sketchbook discussions, 42–43

Hats, 58
Home art, 107–11
Homework assignments, 119–20, 121

Ideas. *See* Art ideas
Independence
  in art evaluation. *See* Self-
    evaluation
  encouraging student, 17, 20,
    23–26, 118–22
  sketchbooks and encouragement
    of, 38–43
Individuality
  in contemporary approach to art
    instruction, 5

Individuality (*continued*)
  in traditional approach to art
      instruction, 5, 6
Inflatables, 58
Investigation, preliminary play and,
    70–72

Keys, 58
Kitchen tools, 58

Lesson plans, 97–138
  art classroom and, 63, 67
  departures from, 61
  ending the lesson and, 126–32
  evaluation of, as work of art,
      132–33
  homework assignments and,
      119–21
  limitations of traditional, 5
  planning for art discussions in,
      122–24
  planning for independent work
      and, 118–22
  play in, 25–26, 69–70, 75,
      102–3
  sample, 133–38
  selecting idea for lesson, 100–2
  selecting play idea for, 102–3
  sketchbooks in, 98, 103, 104
  source of ideas for, 106–15
  student involvement in
      developing, 5–7
  studying other artists and, 60–61,
      124–25
  study of use of, 3–4
  timing and sequencing in,
      115–18
  visual approach to, 103–6, 133
Library, classroom, 59–61
Light bulbs, 58
Line
  importance of, 75–76
  in play, 67, 76–78, 81–83

Magnification, 153
Mapping, 149
Masks, 58, 93, 94
Materials, 50, 51–55
  contemporary art, 9
  environmental search for, 28,
      52–54, 112–15
  methods of investigating, 34–37
  movement and, 78–79
  in play, 75
  shopping for, as source of art
      ideas, 30–33, 111–13
  student selection of, 6–7, 34–37
  study of form and, 87
  surfaces as, 52
  teacher selection of, 6–7
  tools as, 52
  in traditional art teaching, 29
Memorabilia, 58
Mirrors, 58, 153
Mistakes, 131
Movement
  line and, 77–78
  play based on, 78–83
  teacher as performer and, 51,
      89–96
Multimedia experiences, 11, 13
Music, 81

Nagy, John, 114
Natural objects, 58, 59
Nonverbal communication, 49–50,
    165, 174

Observation, shopping and, 32
Office supplies, as art materials,
    35–37
Oldenberg, Claes, 89

Packaging, form and, 86–87
Painting, 49
  on canvas, 14–15

color and, 84–85
movement and, 78, 82
sources of art ideas for, 30–31
unusual methods of, 92
Pantomime, 83, 92
Paper, 58
Parents, sketchbooks and, 43
Penmanship, 49, 76, 81
Performance, 51, 89–96
  artworks in, 129
  examples of themes for, 94–96
  as sculpture activity, 83
Photocopies, 149
Piaget, Jean, 7
Planning
  for discussion of art, 122–24
  importance of, in art process,
    26–27, 97
  lesson. *See* Lesson plans
  role of sketchbooks in, 40–42, 98,
    103
  time management in, 44–45,
    115–18
Plastics, 58, 101
Play, 51, 67–89
  art ideas and, 25–26, 69–70, 75,
    102–3
  as basis of lesson plans, 25–26,
    69–70, 75, 102–3
  block, 49, 134–35
  classroom design and, 66–67
  color in, 67, 83–85, 93
  in display of art objects,
    56–57
  environment encouraging, 10,
    67–69
  fantasy in, 71, 72–75, 102–3
  form and, 87–89
  line in, 67, 75–78
  movement, 78–83
  performance by teachers and,
    91–96
  preliminary, 70–72, 76, 79, 81,
    84–85, 133
  sculpture and, 15–16

selection of idea for, in lesson
    planning, 102–3
  sources of lesson ideas based on,
    106–11
Playing doctor, 135–36
Playing store, 137–38
Plumbing fixtures and equipment,
    58
Preliminary play, 70–72, 133
  color exercises as, 84–85
  dance as, 81
  with linear materials, 76
  movement in, 79
Preparation
  for class, by students, 4–6
  importance of, in art, 4, 6
Printed art, 58
Print making, 52, 100–1
  movement exercises and, 82–83
Problem-solving, sketchbooks in,
    41–42
Projections, 152–53

Redrawing, 128
Reduction, 151
Reproductions, 59–61, 101
Rhodes, Zandra, 59
Role playing, 129
  self-evaluation through, 147–48
  by teacher, 92–93
Rubbings, 148–49
Rulers, 34, 58, 77

Sandbox play, 49
Scales, 58
Sculpture, 60
  classroom modification and,
    67
  dance as form of, 83
  displays of, 56
  movement and, 78
  setups in, 15–16
  sources of art ideas for, 31, 32

Self-evaluation, 139–53
    conversations with peers in, 19,
        140–42, 146–47
    drama in, 147–48
    getting a new perspective and,
        152–53
    imitational techniques in, 148–52
    reviewing of progress of work in,
        139–40
    by teachers, 132–33
    verbal approach to, 140, 143–46
    visual approach to, 140, 146
Setups, 13–16, 109
Shopping
    as source of art ideas, 30–33,
        111–13
Show-and-tell sessions, 37, 53,
    133
Silverman, Ronald H., 6–7
Simplicity, importance of, 104–6,
    151–52
Size, in play, 71
Sketchbooks, 38–43
    encouraging use of, 39–40
    format of, 38–39
    implementing use of, 42–43
    in lesson-planning process, 98,
        103, 104
    role of, 38
    variations on concept of, 120–21
Sound, 94–95
Souvenirs, 58
Space, restructuring classroom,
    62–67
Speed, in play, 71, 74, 115–16
Stampers, 58
Stencils, 77
Stickers, 34, 58
Students
    artistic independence of, 17, 20,
        23–26, 118–22
    class preparation by, 4–6
    conversation between teachers
        and, 166–67, 169
    decision making by, 3–7

    evaluation of art by. See
        Self-evaluation
    inner exploration by, 27
    knowledge of work of other
        artists, 60–61, 124–25
    role in planning art lessons, 27
Subjects, of contemporary art, 7–8,
    11–14
Surfaces, 52
    art classroom, 53–55, 65–66
    color and, 84
    form and, 88
    in movement exercises, 81–83

Teachers, 9–10, 12, 161–71
    art discussion and, 19, 166–67, 169
    as artists, 91, 161–66
    decision making by, 3–7
    encouraging student
        independence, 17, 20, 23–26,
        118–22
    experimentation and, 44
    lesson plans of. See Lesson plans
    limitations of traditional lesson
        plans and, 5
    as mentors and colleagues, 166–71
    performances by, 51, 89–96
    role of, as innovators, 10, 23–26,
        71–72, 174
    role playing by, 92–93
    selection of art ideas by, 6–7
    sharing of environmental search
        by, 30–33
    show-and-tell sessions and, 37, 53,
        133
    student sketchbooks and, 38–43
    traveling art, 62–64
Teaching methods
    for contemporary art, 7–16
    traditional, 1–7
Television, 113–14
Thiebaud, Wayne, 89
Thinking, importance of, 4, 6
Time management, 44–45

importance of, 117–18
in lesson plans, 115–18
Tin containers, 58
Tools
  body parts as, 77–78
  for drawing, 31
  freedom in use of, 81–83
  line-making, 77
  movement and, 78–83
  for painting, 30–31
  searching environment for, 112–15
  selection of, 52
  varying uses of, 34–35
Toys, 58, 59, 75, 107–11
Tracings, 149–50
Transformation, art as, 69–70,
  136–37

University of Kentucky
  Gallery Internship Program, 153,
    154–55
  Gallery Owners Program, 153,
    155–58
  Kentucky Exhibition Models, 153,
    154

Verbal skills
  in communication of art ideas,
    140, 143–46
  imaginative use of language,
    73–74
  play and, 92
  visual skills versus, 47–49
Video production, 114, 146
  projections of work in, 152–53
Vision extenders, 57, 61
Visualization
  importance of, 4
  in lesson planning, 103–6,
    133
  movement and, 78
  planning of art process and,
    26–27

Walls
  alteration of classroom, 65
  classroom display areas on,
    53–54
Windows
  classroom display areas on, 53,
    54–55

About the Author

George Szekely studied at the High School of Music and Art in New York City, The Cooper Union, New York University, Pratt Institute, and Columbia University. He has taught at the City University of New York, and in the New York City public schools. Presently, Dr. Szekely is Area Head of the Department of Art at the University of Kentucky. He has had 12 one-man shows in New York City, has exhibited in major galleries in the United States and Europe, and is the author of *A Study of a Community: Staten Island Architecture and Environment* and *Music and Art in the Elementary School*.